The Triumph of the Black Church

Written by
Elijah L. Hill, Th.B., MBA

TO: HADLEY Mitchell, thanks
for your love for God & his
Holy Word. I appreciate
your support of my 06/20/2013
ministry.
Elijah L. Hill

The Triumph of the Black Church

TABLE OF CONTENTS

DEDICATION

This book is dedicated to three individuals that have been significant in my spiritual journey: my biological father, Ernest E. Hill; my spiritual father, Pastor Mack Reed; and my spiritual mother in the gospel: Missionary Naomi V. Lewis who all live in Omaha, Nebraska where I grew up.

My mother, Mary M. Johnson, was the fourth person of great influence within my spiritual journey. My biological mother Mary Madeline Murphy was born on December 12, 1938, in Kenansville, North Carolina. In my last book, *Women Come Alive*, she was the sole individual mentioned within my dedication.

My spiritual mother in the Gospel Missionary, Naomi V. Lewis, who was my prayer partner kept me focused on fasting and prayer and seeking God between the ages of sixteen and twenty. She encouraged me to maintain my spiritual chase after God. She grew up in the sanctified church, called Robinson Memorial Church of God in Christ, the mother church for the Church of God in Christ in the state of Nebraska. Her family, the McClarity's, was one of the earlier pioneering families of the first Church of God in Christ in Omaha, Nebraska. Her parents are Willie and Lean McClarity.

Missionary Naomi V. Lewis grew up as a little girl at Robinson Memorial Church of God in Christ. The founders of that church were Pastor Edward Robinson and Mother Lizzie Robinson the founder and the national supervisor of women ministry for the Churches of God in Christ, Inc. Naomi would see Bishop Charles Harrison Mason when he would come to Omaha to visit the Robinsons. The healing, deliverance and prayer and fasting ministry of the founder was a part of her upbringing that she imbedded in my spirit.

She encouraged me to know God for myself and to seek his face until His Word came alive within my heart. She believed that I had to seek God and study His Word until revelation knowledge fell from my anointed lips that could effectively feed God's people. I remember she would tell me, "Elijah Hill don't get up there speaking behind that pulpit like these other ministers. They speak dead and dry words because they are delivering God's word in self, rather than allowing themselves to know God deep enough to access His anointing and power."

Missionary Lewis was a woman that believed in prayer with the manifestation of God's supernatural power. She encouraged me in this direction spiritually from the age of fifteen years old until I was about twenty. One day she read to me a letter she had written to a political personality. Her writing ability was so graceful and powerful, so I asked God to give me that gift in my own uniqueness. I had never in my life seen words fall across a page so gracefully and with such clarity.

I spoke with the owner and editor of the Christian Service Network Publishers and he read this manuscript. He told me that out of all his 50 years of editing and ghost writing for some of the most popular ministry personalities. He had only seen one other person outside of me that wrote with such descriptiveness and clarity in telling a story. Therefore, in this dedication I acknowledge one of the most powerful individuals I know with a pen in Omaha, Nebraska, who caused me to strive for excellence and effectiveness in my writing, Missionary Naomi V. Lewis, my mother in the Gospel.

My father in the Gospel, Pastor Mack Reed, to whom I owe a great acknowledgement, was the individual who mentored me from the age of sixteen through these thirty-five years of ministry. He was the closest thing to a 'Paul and Timothy experience' I have ever had in my life.

Pastor Mack Reed of Holy Ghost Temple Church of God in Christ, in Omaha, Nebraska, encouraged me to study other intellectual and knowledgeable sources as well as the Bible. He was an avid self-taught reader and encouraged me to read theology books of all kinds when I was still in high school. He told me he only had a third-grade education, and he inspired me to seek knowledge and take advantage of my education so I could be an effective and knowledgeable speaker as a man of God.

I spent many hours with Pastor Reed between the ages of sixteen and twenty talking about the etiquette, mannerisms and protocol of being a preacher. He taught me how to dress and how to speak to great leaders within the religious community. For four years, I sat at his feet as Paul did Gamaliel in the New Testament. I had the opportunity to absorb his wisdom about being a preacher because he literally believed it to be an art form.

I would go to his house and see books everywhere. He would tell me to read books about homiletics, eschatology and hermeneutics, if I was going to be a minister of the Gospel. He told me I must learn to read. He recommended Eerdman's Commentary as one of the best study aids for developing sermons.

Today Pastor Mack Reed is retired at eighty-one years old. When I was sixteen Pastor Reed told me, "Well, son, I am fifty years old. That means I am on the top of the hill getting ready to go down the hill, and you in your twenties are coming up that same hill. I can teach you something if you listen. Every man has a sphere of influence every man no matter who he is. Always remember to respect every man's influence because you never know when you will need it."

My biological father, Ernest Eugene Hill, was born on December 7, 1937, in Batesville, Arkansas, to Hershel Hill and Clemintine Magness. When Hershel and Clementine met and, she became pregnant with my father Ernest she was only sixteen years. When she was pregnant with my father, her father felt she was too young to marry. My father told me he never knew his father because his mother and her family relocated from the Arkansas area to Omaha, Nebraska.

He met His father, Hershel Hill, later in his youth on two or three occasions when his family went down annually to Little Rock, Arkansas, to visit their friends and relatives. My father told me that my grandfather, Hershel Hill, lived in Little Rock, Arkansas most of his life.

My father Ernest Hill has been not just a father, but also one of my best friends during my life's journey. He has given me great insight and revelation surrounding the strong spiritual gift of insight that was a part of him and his family. My father and I are identical from a spiritual-gift perspective. As we talked over the years, he has sharpened me as Paul did Timothy spiritually and encouraged me to stir-up this gift within me.

The Author of this book Elder Elijah L. Hill

ABOUT THE AUTHOR

Pastor Hill is a native of Omaha, Nebraska, and has been ordained in the gospel ministry for over thirty-five years, and has traveled extensively throughout the United States speaking and sharing with diverse audiences during the course of his ministry. In September 1991 in Omaha, Nebraska, Bishop Louis Henry Ford and several members of their national General Board held a press conference with the media, and Bishop Ford made the following statement to the *Omaha World Herald Newspaper*: "Omaha can do more to bring us back to where we want to go than any other city in America. That's because the (church's) roots are so deeply planted and woven together here." He stated this fact was because Omaha was home to Lizzie Robinson who Ford said was one of the church's pioneering ladies, and he stated that Robinson helped the denomination's founder Bishop Charles H. Mason organize and structure the church.

After this, the Bishop of Nebraska, Vernon Richardson, appointed Elder Elijah Hill as State Historian and Cultural Anthropologist of Nebraska to develop a plan to research and preserve the legacy of Mother Lizzie Robinson who lived in Omaha, Nebraska. She was the first General Supervisor appointed by the Founder of the Church of God in Christ in 1911. He identified and researched her properties that were significant to her history in Omaha and the surrounding area. Elder Hill implemented and conducted research in order to negotiate with the City's Landmarks Heritage Preservation Commission to historically landmark her life story as significant to the history of the State of Nebraska. He also participated in public hearings and meetings to support the first Church of God in Christ to be historically landmarked. He also wrote the nomination for the Federal Registry of historic places that identified Mother Lizzie Robinson's local properties and history as significant to America's history.

Hill implemented the first street named after a woman in the state of Nebraska. Within the Church of God in Christ, denomination he is one of two personalities to get street name changes on behalf of the Church of God in Christ organization's two founding personalities Bishop Charles Harrison Mason and Mother Lizzie Robinson. The other was the former Presiding Bishop Louis Henry Ford for Bishop Charles Harrison Mason in 1958. Presiding Bishop Louis Henry Ford gave Elder Hill a proclamation from the Presiding Bishop Office in Memphis, Tennessee, for preserving the heritage of the Church of God in Christ on behalf of our founding personalities in their church history in 1992. In 1993, the Governor of the State of Nebraska recognized Elder Hill for the renaissance of Mother Lizzie Robinson's history. Her history is a part of Nebraska's history of nationally known personalities that had a global humanitarian influence in the world.

The National Trust for Historic Preservation recognized Elder Hill for Historic Preservation as a national preservationist in urban America in 1993. He was also historian for the late Bishop E. Harris Moore of Western Missouri, who served as Assistant Chair of National Church of God in Christ Hospital Fund in 1995. In 2002, Elder Hill served Bishop Emmanuel Newton, Bishop of Western Missouri he served as National Chair of Elders Council of the Church of God in Christ.

Hill developed curriculum for the national training institute in Memphis, Tennessee, from 1994 to 2003, on the topic of Bishop Charles Harrison Mason's historic leadership secrets. These annual classes are for leaders within the national organization that seek for more information surrounding the Church of God in Christ organization's corporate culture. The class takes place during the Holy Convocation, and attendees come from throughout the United States to take these courses.

The mayor of Omaha, Nebraska, appointed Elijah Hill to be a part of the City of Omaha, Nebraska's, local Landmarks Commission. His duties were to hold public hearings in the City of Omaha's place of business, to oversee the city's inventory of $100 million dollars' worth of historic properties and to oversee public forums for the mayor and his committee maintained and reviewed if historic properties were significant as a source of the city's civic and cultural pride for future generations. His committee's duties were to designate, preserve, protect, and enhance the perpetuation of the city's historical structures to maintain their heritage. Elder Hill, because of his work in propelling the Church of God in Christ to civic visibility locally became the first and youngest African American appointed to the City's Landmarks Heritage Preservation Commission. He implemented and spearheaded the Landmarks Heritage Preservation Commission's first use of Roberts Rules of Orders for holding public meetings in the City of Omaha, Nebraska.

Elder Elijah Hill, spending hours of research in his cultural anthropological findings and archives was able to contribute several historical books for the Church of God in Christ. He has authored and published seven books on different topics on the Bible. They include *Angels, Who was Satan in Heaven and His Earthly Works,* and *Who was Christ Before He Came to Earth?* He later wrote a book on Eschatology called *The Unsealing of the Last Things* (Bible Prophecy), and *Women Come Alive* (The historical biography of Lizzie Robinson). He also wrote on the biography of Bishop William J. Seymour called *The Azusa Street Revival Wrapped in Swaddling Clothes Lying in a Manger, and Women Come Alive Historic Photo Album* and *The Great Cloud of Witnesses Early Bishops' Historic Album.*

It was in 2005 he completed his first scholarly writing completing the biography of Mother Lizzie Robinson, the only book on the First General Supervisor's life story. In 2007, he produced another historic photo album during the 100-year centennial celebration of the Church of God in Christ on all the women in the national church appointed by Mother Lizzie Robinson. In 2008, he released another photo album of over 200 pictures of all the appointed Bishops by Bishop Charles Harrison Mason from the beginning of the church until the seventies. In 2013, he has now completed an extensive work on the life of

11

Bishop Charles Harrison Mason entitled *The Triumph of the Black Church.* Elder Hill has been a contributory writer for the *Whole Truth Magazine* on several occasions for Dr. David Hall, Sr., and he has written for the Church of God in Christ Publishing House for the Young People Willing Workers writing and developing curriculum for Bishop Whitehead and their national quarterly publication.

Elder Hill has had several national endorsements during his 20-year writing career. Elder Hill's book on biblical prophecy, *The Unsealing of The Last Things,* was endorsed by the following in 1993: Presiding Bishop Chandler David Owens as the head of the Church of God in Christ Worldwide, Dr. Oliver J. Haney, Jr., past Dean of C.H. Mason Theological Seminary, Interdenominational Theological Center, Atlanta, GA; General Board member and founder of West Angeles Church of God in Christ, Los Angeles, CA; Bishop Charles E. Blake; and Bishop Richard J. White (Mr. Clean) then National President of the Evangelism for the Church of God in Christ.

The Assemblies of God's *Enrichment Magazine* dedicated to 100 years of Pentecostalism in America highlighted Rev. Elijah L. Hill's book, *Women Come Alive.* Out of the twenty books reviewed it was noted as of the important books to read for Pentecostals, and reviewed by two staff members of the Assemblies of God's Theological Seminary Dr. Deborah Gill head of Women's Issue in the AG denomination, and James H. Riley, Jr. In 2006 another review of the book *Women Come Alive* directed by the *Whole Truth* magazine, the National Magazine for the Church of God in Christ Worldwide, and the reviewer was the noted scholar on women's issues Dr. Adrienne M. Israel, professor of History and intercultural studies at Guilford College.

Elder Hill is the current president of the COGICMuseum.org the first electronic museum introduced to the Church of God in Christ in 2007, which documented and electronically chronicled as a cultural anthropologist the history of the church of God in Christ On-Line. He implemented a digital record keeping system of management of Mother Lizzie

Robinson's collection, archiving her collection of 100 books and 700 photos. His dedication with digitally making these files available for his next project, The Church of God in Christ Encyclopedia Project, where individuals can submit documentation online to provide a printed collection of COGIC pioneers that have contributed such as deacons, elders, mothers, jurisdictional leaders and national leaders who have had an impact on the Church of God in Christ history. Elder Hill has dedicated his doctoral degree in Organizational Leadership to the electronic archiving and the preservation of the first fifty years of the Church of God in Christ Pre-Civil Rights history. This finished academic work will share a new body of knowledge for scholars throughout the world so they can identify and highlight the advancement of the Church of God in Christ's use of best practices in archiving their history.

In 1989, Elder Hill went on a three day fast and had a vision of Bishop Charles Harrison Mason, founder of the Church of God in Christ and Mother Lizzie Robinson. In this vision, he saw Bishop Mason and Mason told him to preserve the history of the old pioneers of his movement. That day the Lord spoke to him to go over to Pastor Vernon Richardson's house and let him know he would be the Bishop of Nebraska in the next eight months. The national church was to come back to Omaha, Nebraska, to say who would be the Bishop. The Presiding Bishop Louis Henry Ford came back in eight months and selected Bishop Vernon Richardson as Bishop of Nebraska just as God had revealed to him in the vision. In 1999, Elder Hill was on a five-day fast and sent Presiding Bishop Chandler David Owens a prophetic letter that he was sick in his body, but that God was going to heal him completely. It was later in 2000 that Presiding Bishop Owens acknowledged he was sick acknowledged his healing of cancer after his surgery. The accuracy of the prophecy for Presiding Bishop Owens blessed him so he endorsed his Elder Hill's book on biblical prophecy, *The Unsealing of the Last Things.* Elder Hill wrote several prophetic letters to Presiding Bishop Owens, Presiding Bishop G.E. Patterson and Presiding Bishop Charles E. Blake that he kept secret since the letters had to do with future direction for the national church. Now after 20 years he has now made them public on his Church of God in Christ historical discussions blog http://www.blog.cogicmuseum.org.

Elder Hill prophesied that the national church should update their April meeting by electronically automating registration in 1999, so that individuals would not have to wait in long lines. The national secretary would implement it the late Dr. A.Z. Hall, who agreed with this idea, and start its implementation before he passed.

Dr. A. Z. Hall had a great respect for Elder Hill. They met at Faust Temple Church of God in Christ in Jacksonville in 1982 when Elder Hill spoke for Pastor Faust on Sunday morning where Dr. Hall was a deacon at the time.

In 2001 during 911, Elder Hill shared a prophetic letter with the then-President of the United States, President George Bush, revealing a strategy to deal with future attacks on America. During the Anthrax issue, Elder Hill shared spiritually with the President how to utilize herbal composition to counteract its harmful effects. Elder Hill also shared his book, *The Unsealing of the Last Things* with President Bush. He encouraged him to look to the religious community for direction in dealing with the Mideast before making a military decision. The President called for several religious leaders (including the late Presiding Bishop G. E. Patterson) to come to Washington to help him understand the biblical approach to the Mideast. The President sent back correspondence to Elder Hill appreciating his input during 911, and the insight that he gave during this of crisis time in America.

In 2001, Elder Hill wrote a prophetic letter to the Presiding Bishop Gilbert Earl Patterson surrounding the direction to leading the church and Elder Hill said that he should include the history of the church, sharing with him ten ways to implement it. Presiding Bishop Patterson quickly implemented an idea produced a CD with him and Bishop Charles Harrison Mason's praying together, and he introduced it during the next called meeting of the Church of God in Christ in April of 2000. He later implemented the *Old Time Way* songs, which became a success to all of Christendom in America.

In 2003, Elder Hill prophesied that Bishop T.D. Jakes would in the future begin to develop other Potter's Houses that would evolve from his ministry. Within five years later there implementation come to past in 2013 there are now four Potters Houses. In 2007, Elder Hill shared a prophetic letter to the entire Church of God in Christ prophesying thirty days before the Holy Convocation "it was God's will that Bishop Charles E. Blake become the next Presiding Bishop of the COGIC." Thirty days later the Lord brought it to pass. January 2012, a year before it occurred, Elder Hill prophesied on Facebook that the current President of the United States, Barack Obama, would win a second term. However, many in the media as well as the religious sector stated it would not happen, in November of 2012 this came to pass.

Elder Hill graduated in 1999 with a Masters of Business Administration and a Masters in Educational Technology at MidAmerica Nazarene University in Olathe, Kansas. He is currently attending Grand Canyon University for his doctoral degree in Organizational Leadership with an emphasis in organizational development. His electronic biographical and chronological accomplishments are online at blog.cogicmuseum.org or by googling his name, Elijah L. Hill.

PREFACE

The Triumph of the Black Church will review and distinguish the factors and specific actions that lead to the success of Bishop Charles Harrison Mason as an African American religious organization's change leader in the beginning 20th Century Pentecostal Movement as it relates to his First Amendment rights of the Freedom of Religion in the Constitution of the United States. He approached the United States government during World War I's 1917 Selective Service (Draft) law to negotiate his organization's civil liberties as Christians to uphold their religious freedom as conscientious objectors to World War I's military draft laws.

The purpose of this historical narrative is to describe how during the Jim Crow system in America, this small newly-formulated African American denomination and their national leader Bishop Charles Harrison Mason, faced seemingly insurmountable governmental harassment, persecution, and criminal prosecution from 1917-1920 for requesting religious liberties exemption and succeeded in court during World War I's Selective Service military draft laws.

One of the more important legal issues that legal scholars continue to dispute over is the First Congress's original meaning of the First Amendment Free Exercise Clause (Muñoz, 2008). It is important to note that historically America has had great challenges during wartime relating to the rule of constitutional law surrounding the violation of First Amendment rights of its citizens. The most repressive of these times was during World War I in 1918 when Congress created the Sedition Act of 1918 (Holmes, 2005).

It is critical to note that historically during every national wartime event in America's history from the American Revolution of 1776 up to President George W. Bush's famous, "War on Terrorism," that blended constitutional law with governmental regulations to justify censorship of America's freedom of speech justified by the need to protect America's national security (Holmes, 2005).

It is important to uphold the purity of the guarantees of the First Amendment that true democracy must rest upon, not the rule of men, but upon the rule of our constitutional law (Giannella, 1967). Therefore, it is upon this premise historically called the Church-State Law, that the scholar Tamm (1999) argues will be the main foundation. He stated that the opening words of the First Amendment to the U. S. Constitution states, "Congress shall make no law respecting an establishment of religion, or prohibiting the free exercise thereof;..."(p. 253) preceding even the great freedoms of speech, press, and the freedom of religious assembly.

The beginning of World War I and the beginning of the creation of the Selective Service for the United States of America, also known as the Draft took place in 1917. This meant that American citizens that were male over the age of eighteen years old had to volunteer to enlist in the military service to defend America as a nation during wartime. The scholars Schlabach & Hughes (1987) describe in 1917 the President of the United States Woodrow Wilson's statement surrounding exemptions under religious liberties in time of war, he stated, "members of a well-recognized religious sect or organization that had a creed prohibiting war service were eligible, but they still had to perform noncombatant military service" (p. 60).

The Federal Bureau of Investigation (FBI) files (1918) cite that Bishop Charles Harrison Mason in 1917 sent a telegram to the President of the United States to request audience concerning his organization to negotiate his religious organizations tenets relating to receiving an exemption surrounding religious liberty. The FBI files revealed that Mason went to Washington, DC, met with the War Department in 1917, and shared the religious tenets of his national African American Religious organizations, including that the shedding of blood was against the Pentecostal Protestant faith of the Churches of God in Christ that they were pacifist. After this meeting in Washington D. C., Bishop Charles Harrison Mason's

Pentecostal religious organization became one of the first Protestant and Pentecostal organizations to become exempt by President Woodrow Wilson's War Department in 1917.

The Churches of God in Christ drew up a statement that they gave to their denomination's members to submit to the local Selective Service boards throughout the United States of America. It was in Lexington, Mississippi, 1918 that the local officials became insulted and upset that Negros coming from plantations could tell them that they did not have to participate in the war because of the religious liberties granted to the Churches of God in Christ.

The FBI files cite that the Lexington, Mississippi, clerk of the court contacted the FBI with allegations that Bishop Charles Harrison Mason was leading Negros in the South to be refuter's and deserters of the Selective Service of the United States of America. Mason while he was in Lexington, MS, was arrest and he was placed in the Lexington jail then later sent to federal prison and booked for allegedly committing treason against the United States government under the Sedition Act of 1918.

During this time Bishop C. H. Mason's African American Pentecostal organization had within its ranks many white members, not just black members. Many white ministers were holding Mason's credentials and used his licensing name, the Church of God in Christ. Local governments recognized his organization's credentials and ministers that had his licensing could get discounts on train travel. Therefore, thousands of whites, as well as blacks looked up to Mason as one of the fathers of the Pentecostal movement and they supported his conscientious objector stance during World War I.

The FBI files noted that Mason's organization was practicing in multicultural worship because white men held major roles within his African American organization and followed his leadership. The FBI felt that this was in violation of Jim Crow laws in America, and the Plessy vs. Ferguson legislation of 1896. I have observed through my research that in actuality, Bishop Charles Harrison Mason is a missing part of America's history relating to pre-civil rights in America. Additionally, that Mason's life and work predated Dr. Martin Luther King's Civil Rights Movement by institutionalizing interracial interaction between white and blacks from his revivals in 1894-1950's right on the wake of Plessy vs. Ferguson (1896) that gave support to segregation in America. It is historically important to note that Dr. Martin Luther King gave his famous 1968 last speech, *I've Been to The Mountain Top,* the day before his assassination at Bishop Charles Harrison Mason's World Headquarter building in Memphis, Tennessee, where Mason was one of those first African American leaders entombed at his world headquarters location.

In Paris, Texas, in 1919, the grand jury trial of Bishop Charles Harrison Mason took place. However, the Judge threw out the Federal government's case of treason because the rescinding Seditious Act of 1918 by Congress, which agreed that it was a mistake violating the constitution of the United State's rule regarding freedom of religion that no law shall be made by Congress irrespective of religious freedom in America (Holmes, 2005).

The Triumph of the Black Church will reveal through the extraordinary life story of Bishop Charles Harrison Mason a true early twentieth century change leader from 1896-1961. He as an African American religious leader who implemented an innovative approach by standing upon his First Amendment constitutional law under freedom of religion contradicting Plessy vs. Ferguson in 1896 that supported segregation in America. The nation of America had its long struggle surrounding slavery and racism from the time of the Missouri Compromise of 1820, which stopped slavery from expanding beyond Midwestern and northern United States. The Kansas-Nebraska Act of 1855 repealed the Missouri Compromise of 1820 demonstrating America's confusion surrounding slavery giving the settlers that option to choose rather to have slaves or not. In June 17, 1858, it was at the Republican National Convention that Abraham Lincoln then only an Illinois state senator proposed a new vision for America. In his speech historically it is known the, "House Divided Speech," that would be the beginning of changing the mind-set of Republicans to oppose the new Kansas-Nebraska Act of 1855 and eventually slavery in America. During this time, it was not popular for African American leaders to make a public stand on their religious beliefs in civic equality of human rights without the threat of lynching. It does not matter what your race or the color of your skin is under the constitution of the United States. Under the constitution of the United States, everyone has the right to pursue freedom to assemble fellowshipping with other races or the religious right to refuse to take up arms during war as conscientious objectors to invoke the freedom of their religion.

References

Giannella, D. A. (1967). Religious Liberty, Nonestablishment, and Doctrinal Development. *Harvard Law Review, 80*(7), 1381.

Holmes, S. (2005). Dismal Precedents. *New Republic, 232*(7), 31-37.

Lovett, L. (1973). Perspective on the black origins of the contemporary Pentecostal movement. *Journal Of The Interdenominational Theological Center*, (1), 36-49.

Muñoz, V. (2008). The Original Meaning of the Free Exercise Clause: The Evidence From The First Congress. *Harvard Journal of Law & Public Policy, 31*(3), 1083-1120.

Tamm, R. (1999). Religion Sans Ultimate: A Re-Examination of Church-State Law. *Journal Of Church & State, 41*(2), 253-284.

U.S. War Department & Federal Bureau of Investigation Files, Charles H. Mason Files Investigation Violating the Espionage Act.

Chapter 1—Experiencing God's Presence as a Child

It was September 1864 in Tennessee just outside of Memphis on the Prior Farm Plantation, and the fall harvest had just begun for the ex-slaves on the plantation. A year earlier, the Civil War ended with President Abraham Lincoln's signing of the Emancipation Proclamation; the proclamation declared, "That all persons held as slaves" within the rebellious states "are, and henceforward shall be free." Many of the ex-slaves did not know where to go or what to do, but they knew they were free. Their slave masters, for many months, announced that they were free, but many decided to stay on the plantation to make their living. Historically, some slaves did choose to leave the South with their families and travel to the North to make their way in a completely new world: taking the risk to remove themselves from their old land of bondage. Still, others became sharecroppers that were tenants on the land, and paid their rent by tending to their white owners crops. This was a very good trade off, since tending to the crops on the farm was their only occupational specialty.

On the Prior Farm, Jerry and Eliza Mason were one of the ex-slave families that decided to remain on the master's land as sharecropper, in order to raise their family to make a living.[1] The Mason family were strong adherents to the Baptist religion and members of the Mt. Helm Missionary Baptist Church. The church was a great source of strength to them as it was for most African Americans, during and after the Civil War.[2]

Eliza Mason converted to Christianity during this dark period of slavery. She gave her whole heart to the Lord, and at every opportunity, would steal away with other slaves to pray for the evils of their diabolically, oppressive situation in the South.

Bishop Charles Harrison Mason

The presence and power of God would be manifested in their midst as these slaves came together mourning and wailing before the Lord to "loose the hand of Pharaoh" in their lives.[3] She developed a gift of prayer that changed lives: not only in these prayer groups, but even in the Mason family home.

Around February of 1866, Eliza discovered that she was pregnant with her fifth child. Before this child, she had four other children: Joseph was the oldest, then Mary, Eliza, and Jeremiah (Jerry). There was also one other child, Israel S. Nelson, the stepson of Jerry Mason.[4] During her daily chores, she found time to spend with the Lord, asking Him to bless her baby, and that the child would know about God's Presence. On September 8, 1866, a year after the Civil War ended, she gave birth to a beautiful baby boy. Jerry and Eliza decided they would name him Charles Harrison Mason. Little did they realize their baby boy would become one of the most influential churchman of the 20th Century in America?

Eliza wanted little Charlie to know God's presence, even as a toddler. She desired to impress upon him the necessity of prayer and reverencing the God of heaven by practicing a lifestyle of prayer before him. [5] And she recalled the Scriptures found in I Samuel 1:27-28, *For this child I prayed; and the LORD hath given me my petition which I asked of him: Therefore, also I have lent him to the LORD; as long as he liveth, he shall be lent to the LORD. And he worshipped the LORD there."* This is the story of Hannah, dedicating the child (Samuel) she prayed for, back to the Lord. Like Hannah, Eliza would also see her desires fulfilled, as she took young Charlie to the fervent prayer meetings with the old ex-slaves. The older ones talked about having a "strong prayer religion," and this is what she yearned for her son to have. In addition, at the age of seven, as he joined his mother in earnest prayer to obtaining this "strong prayer religion" the old ones spoke of, he began to experience the presence of God. [6] This experience eventually inspired a divine purpose on his life: stated in the *Pentecostal Encyclopedia:*

"Mason, who viewed his lifelong task as one of simply preserving "the spiritual" and "prayer tradition" of the black religious experience." [7]

These religious experiences set him apart from the other neighborhood children.[8] He spent more time with the older crowd, for he seemed to learned more while being in their presence than with children of his own age.[9]

God began to deal with him through dreams and visions as a young child. He demonstrated supernatural characteristics that were evident to all that knew him. It appeared that God was fulfilling his mother's dreams because Charlie began to develop his own "prayer religion," tarrying before God until he got an answer from him.[10] The people in his community were a close-knit group; together they served God and encouraged Charlie (from the age of 7 to 13) to continue to allow God to use him.

In similitude to the child Samuel ministering to the Lord (I Samuel 2:18), little Charlie became known as the young Samuel of his community, as he grew up before the presence of the Lord. He started early in the path of spending time with God in prayer as a vital part of his salvation and Christian experience. When Charles got older, he would spend hours on his knees in prayer before God to deliver his people.

In 1878, when Charles Harrison Mason was twelve years old, a yellow fever epidemic devastated the Prior Farm Community. Many died as a result of this outbreak, and his father decided to take his family as far away as possible-to Plumerville, Arkansas.[11] Jerry and his family had made it through the evils of American Slavery and the Civil War in the South, and he was not about to lose them to this terrible plague. He did not want to leave the Prior Farm where he spent most of his life, but he feared for the life of his wife and children. He had witnessed too many friends losing their spouses and children, so in November of 1878, he reluctantly relocated from Tennessee to Arkansas leaving the only home that Charlie knew as a child.

In 1955, Boston, MA, Church of God in Christ Women's Convention, L-R, Bishop C. H. Mason, Mother Lillian Brooks-Coffey, Mother Letha Herndon.

In 1958, Women's Convention

He heard word about another plantation in Arkansas called the John Watson Plantation, down near a swamp that needed some tenant farmers; [12]

Down in Plumersville, Arkansas Charlie realized that the spiritual environment was the opposite of his original plantation home in Tennessee. The people were not as committed to Christianity at this new location. It was hard for him being around the children that did not understand his spiritual lifestyle. He spent many nights crying because he longed to be back on his family's old homestead in Tennessee. The people in this community were more sinful, and they did not take God seriously. [13] Nevertheless, it was at Plumersville that Charlie began to have dreams and visions of Heaven and Hell. These spiritual experiences caused him to surrender his total life to God more deeply.

In his new home, the opportunity for Charlie's education was almost impossible. His father, working hard for the family, needed his help in the field to harvest the crops. Jerry felt that since Charlie had become old enough, and he needed to assist him with the farming responsibilities.

In August 1880, just before Charlie's fourteenth birthday, he became very sick with a fever and chills. Eliza feared for his life, since so many had died from these symptoms in Tennessee. She cried out to God for the life of her son, but it seemed to no avail. His symptoms grew worse. [14] She tried everything within her power to comfort little Charles. Day and night, he would experience great fevers, and she did what she could to cool his body. During his chills, she placed warm blankets near his bed to warm him. She would have to leave him to go to work in the fields. Her plantation farming duties helped to keep up the rent on their tenant farm. [15]

During these times of Charlie being alone with this dreaded illness, he would pray long like the slaves of old for God to answer his prayer and heal his body. He was so weak that he could not get down on his knees, but he fervently prayed and mourned before the Lord. It seemed as if God was not hearing him as before, so he decided to make sure that his commitment to God was sure before leaving this earth. For he had seen some early dreams and visions of Hell, with these revelations he saw, he didn't want to go there.[16] Mason stated in his testimony in Professor Courts' book, *Lord, I have Done All That I Can Do,* that immediately, the glory and power of God's healing virtue came upon him. As he began to praise God for lifting his burden, his strength returned, and he made haste to get up out of that sick bed. He rejoiced and praised the God of Heaven: skipping along, crying and rejoicing at the same time saying, "Glory to God, hallelujah, praise His holy Name."[17]

Eliza Mason was on her way home from working the fields, and she found that Charlie was not there on his sick bed. She frantically went about wondering what had happened to her son; asking herself if he had died unexpectedly. Then she saw Charles walking along the road coming back towards the house. It was a jubilantly sweet meeting. She was beside herself with joy as he told her of his miraculous healing.[18] She was so happy, that the next Sunday she took Charles to church to be baptized. She took him to the Mt. Olive Missionary Baptist, where Charles' half-brother, I.S. Nelson, was the pastor. The whole church filled with exuberant worship and thanksgiving to God, upon hearing of the miraculous healing of young Charles. The people were amazed that a boy his age had prayed, and God healed the most dreaded disease of their day through his own prayer.[19]

In 1939, Saints arriving at the 32nd Annual Holy Convocation in Memphis, Tennessee.

In 1951, L-R, Bishop C.H. Mason, Mother Lillian Brooks-Coffey, Mary McLeod Bethune, Dr. Arenia Mallory

Tragically, Charlie's father became sick with the yellow fever, and he died on the John Watson's Plantation. His mother was devastated and overwhelmed with sorrow by the death of her husband. Not only did she lose a spouse and companion, but a man that was unconditionally devoted to taking care of her and the children.[20] Charlie sadness by his father's sudden death. He was just a teenager who had just relocated to a new community the he did not like. Now he had to become a man early in his life; working even harder in the fields, and attempting to fill the void left by his father. Alongside his mother and his other siblings, he sometimes worked from sun up to sundown.

Nevertheless, Charles strength was in him praying and trusting in the same God who delivered him from his own life-threatening experience. He became even more intimately knowledgeable of the power of God through his prayer life, and he dedicated his life to praying for others healings. One day at the altar, he accepted his calling to the Christian faith as a lay preacher in the Baptist church his mother attended. He would attend the summer camp meetings all over Arkansas, helping people "pray through" at the mourner's bench. From the age of fourteen to the age of twenty-four, he diligently served at the altar, fervently praying for others. He also traveled to other camp meetings throughout the Arkansas area, giving his personal testimony of how God still heals through the power of prayer.[21]

ENDNOTES

Chapter 1: Experiencing God's Presence as a Child

1. James Courts, The *History and Life Work of Bishop C.H. Mason*, Privately Published: Memphis, TN, 1918, Page 19.
2. Burgess, Stanley M., and McGee, Gary B., *Dictionary of Pentecostal and Charismatic Movements*, Published by Zondervan, Grand Rapids, MI, 1988, Page 585.
3. James Courts, The *History and Life Work of Bishop C.H. Mason*, Privately Published: Memphis, TN, 1918, Page 19.
4. 1870 United States Federal Census, Birth record of Charles H. Mason, in Shelby County, Tennessee, District #7.
5. James Courts, *The History and Life Work of Bishop C.H. Mason*, Privately Published: Memphis, TN, 191, Page 19
6. Burgess, Stanley M., and McGee, Gary B., *Dictionary of Pentecostal and Charismatic Movements*, Published by Zondervan, Grand Rapids, MI, 1988, Page 585.
7. Ibid., Page 587.
8. James Courts, *The History and Life Work of Bishop C.H. Mason*, Privately Published: Memphis, TN, 1918, Page 20.
9. Ibid., 19
10. Burgess, Stanley M., and McGee, Gary B., *Dictionary of Pentecostal and Charismatic Movements*, Published by Zondervan, Grand Rapids, MI, 1988, Page 585.
11. 1880 United States Federal Census, Jerry Mason family relocated to live in Arkansas with wife Eliza Mason and children.
12. James Courts, *The History and Life Work of Bishop C.H. Mason*, Privately Published: Memphis, TN, 1918, Page 20.
13. Ibid., Page 20
14. Bishop Ithiel C. Clemmons, *Bishop C.H. Mason and the roots of the Church of God in Christ*, Publisher: Pneuma Life Publishing, Bakersfield, California, 93389, Page 4.
15. Ibid., Page 4
16. James Courts, *The History and Life Work of Bishop C.H. Mason*, Privately Published: Memphis, TN, 1918, Page 21.
17. Ibid., Page 20
18. Ibid., Page 20
19. Ibid., Page 21
20. Burgess, Stanley M., and McGee, Gary B., *Dictionary of Pentecostal and Charismatic Movements*, Published by Zondervan, Grand Rapids, MI, 1988, Page 586.

21. Bishop Ithiel C. Clemmons, *Bishop C.H. Mason and the Roots of the Church of God in Christ,* Publisher: Pneuma Life Publishing, Bakersfield, California, 93389, Page 5.

Chapter 2—The Test of a Failed Marriage

At the age of twenty-three, Charles Harrison Mason realized that it was his destiny and divine purpose to accept God's ministerial calling upon his life. The Lord had been upon him for some years now and he had already experienced God's presence and power. However, like many men of God before him and after him, he encountered a wonderfully attractive *distraction;* his distraction's name was Alice Saxton. So Young Mason "detoured" from his Godly call to pursue (and eventually marry) the first love of his life.[1]

Now, the meeting of these two wonderful people was not by happenstance. Eliza Mason Charlie's mother was a very close friend of Alice's mother. This brought the two families together often. While Charles was growing up, he grew quite fond of Alice. Ultimately, Charles found that his heart melted toward her and they started going together as young people. The Saxton family loved young Mason and they were aware of Charles and Alice feelings for each other.[2] They knew Charles' mother had raised him well, and that he was a very focused young man that had a promising future. They had no problem embracing him as the young man that would eventually become wedded to their daughter.

Charles Mason decided to put God and his ministerial career on hold and concentrate wholly on winning Ms. Alice Saxton hand in marriage. He told the Lord that he would not go totally into full-time ministry until he had a wife first. His plans were to work to acquire a home, and then devote his time seeking after his choice for a wife. Though he looked at many young promising beautiful women, he unequivocally knew that his final choice would be Alice: for he was deeply in love with her.[3]

Regrettably, his decision to put her before his relationship with God, inevitably wreaked havoc on his prayer life, since he was so consumed with his love for her that he even attempted to bargain with God; thinking that if he could have her, then he would be committed more to God's divine calling on his life.[4]

When it came to choosing a mate, there was another major concern that Charles neglected to consider–spiritual compatibility. Many great men and women of God have fallen into the trap of listening to their flesh, rather than the Spirit of God in choosing a mate. There may be a physical, intellectual, and emotional connection between the two of them, but without a spiritual connection, we are inviting a completely new set of problems and heartaches that will compound the ones that already exist in a marital relationship. However, it was no surprise that Charles chose someone he had no spiritual compatibility with in living his life for Christ. He was already being disobedient in putting Alice before his relationship with God. Matthew 6:33 states, *"But seek ye first the kingdom of God, and his righteousness; and all these things shall be added unto you."* There is nothing wrong with desiring a mate, but a failed relationship is inevitable when we put that individual in a place where God alone should be-first in our hearts.

Too many are willing to compromise their Godly standards once they feel that they are in love with someone. As the saying goes, "love is blind." Our emotions unchecked by the guidelines of God's Word will spin out of control just as Mason's did. He was willing to stop seeking God, and seek after what his flesh desired. This first relationship would end in tragedy, later causing him a lot more harm than good.[5] We can't place our desire for someone over God's will and purpose in your life. Our infatuation will cause us to compromise too many (if not all) of our Godly principles.

Mason finally got what he wanted on January 15, 1890: when he married nineteen-year-old Alice Saxton. Nevertheless, it did not take long for the relationship to start 'going south.' He had told the Lord that he wanted a wife first, before starting full-time ministry. He had not mentioned this *ministry business* to his wife. The more he proceeded to be about his Father's business, the worse his relationship with Alice became she wanted no part in being a minister's wife. She did not want that responsibility, and she let Charles know that she married him, *not* his ministry. She could not relate to Mason's heart for souls, and his desire to preach the Gospel.[6] Note: It does not only matter that your mate is a Christian, it matters that they have the same heart (or vision) toward God that you do.

Whenever he would go to minister, she would always accuse him of being with another woman. She felt that too many preachers were sexually involved with the *sisters* in the church. Even though Charles only loved Alice, she never allowed herself to believe in him or his ministry. This caused a tremendous strain on their marriage this mistrust of him in ministry would be the straw that broke the camel's back of their marital relationship. The adultery she accused him of, eventually is what she fall into herself. After only two years of marriage, she divorced him for another man she had begun to become involved with intimately. Her reason for leaving she told him she did not want to be married to a preacher.[7]

Tragically, too many spouses, knowingly and inadvertently, can hinder the ministries of their mates. Their greatest and most heart-wrenching battles do not occur with the congregation or the world, but within the private life of the individual in ministry. Even, Charles H. Mason (who would one day become one of the most important figures in Pentecostal history) succumbed to the desires of his own flesh and allowed his relationship with the beautiful Alice Saxton, to distract him from his ministry. The disastrous aftermath of these circumstances not only led him to discontinue ministry for an extended period, but it brought him to the point of depression and even contemplated suicide.[8]

Our disobedience can lead us down some dark paths and take us through some horrific trials, but this does not negate God's love for us. To the contrary, the trials we encounter due to disobedience validate God's love for us. Hebrews 12:6 states, *"The Lord disciplines those He loves, and chastises everyone He accepts as a son."* (NIV).

In 1892 when Bishop C.H. Mason

In 1910, Charles Price Jones

Later when Mason remarried, he realized that whomever he chose, he must make sure she supported God's destiny for his ministerial future.[9] He indeed had learned an invaluable lesson about marriage and relationships. The most important thing is that the person is compatible spiritually above all else, assisting you in fulfilling your Godly purpose, versus being an idol you have placed before God and His work.[10] This experience left an indelible mark on the life of Bishop C.H. Mason. It influenced his strong and adamant position in his Biblical teaching that says; *Let every man have his own wife* (I Cor. 7:2). His organization within their older tradition sometimes the older saints would selected mates for individuals who could not discern who the best mate was for them; suggesting that they choose someone strong in their Pentecostal faith. The older mothers were very adamant on the biblical topic of, "not being unequally yoked," with an unbeliever. They knew the pain it would cause those that were new to the faith.

Being married should not be the focus of the believer. There is no need to remind God constantly that we are alone. I believe that this is an insult to Him. Did He not recognize that it was not good for Adam to be alone and made a help "meet" (a helper that was suitable) for him? In other words, He made someone compatible to him (Genesis 2:18). Furthermore, the Lord is the one who brought the mate to Adam (Genesis 2:22). If you are not married yet, God has prepared a mate compatible for you; someone in agreement with your spiritual destiny and work in God's Kingdom. How can two walk together except they be agreed? (Amos 3:3). God knows what we need, concerning a mate and everything else. He is able to give us someone who will walk beside us, promoting, edifying His Kingdom.[11]

Charles Mason tried within his power to make the marriage work, but Alice refused to cooperate. She would separate and leave Mason, attempting to persuade him to cease his preaching ministry.[12] The emotional abuse he received from her tore at his heart, and put him through a plethora of negative, psychological gymnastics. Mason confessed that when Alice came back for short moments, they were really experiencing these circumstances because of his disobedience to God. He had completely stopped preaching the Gospel.[13] Alice divorced Mason, in desperation, Charles cried out to God to help him, but he found no relief in prayer.[14] No matter how diligently he prayed for his marriage to be fixed, his prayers returned void.

Ultimately, Charles repented before God and the church; confessing his disobedience, which led to his failed marriage his belief, was that he was in danger of God's judgment because of him turning his back on God, which resulted in this divorce. He also stated that he was a backslidden preacher that refused to preach because his wife did not want a preacher for a husband was a wrong decision he made. He confessed in church he wanted her so badly that he placed her before God and he lost her anyway because of it.[15] He then began to lay before God in prayer. He reestablished his intercessory commitment to God lying on his face before the Lord, until he felt the Lord's presence again.[16] His relationship with God began to rekindle again.

Charles Harrison Mason began to seek an even deeper experience with the Lord. It was during this period that he came across the famous African American evangelist Amanda Berry's *Holiness Newspaper*.[17] Through reading her writings about the holiness doctrine; he began to come into a greater enlightenment surrounding his present Baptist faith beliefs that were in error of the scriptures. He realized that people needed to live right before God; there was a sanctification process where the Holy Spirit works with the believer to be committed to holy living. In Charles Mason's Baptist belief, teaching of living right or sanctification was missing in his Baptist faith.   This missing information on holiness living according to the Bible was just what he needed to continue rekindling the fire in having a deeper commitment to God. Charles realized that as a Baptist there were certain biblical aspects of the whole true of the bible that was missing. It was at this point that he began to include the Holiness doctrine in his preaching. His desire was to bring the full knowledge of holy living to his Baptist friends in the faith.[18]

ARKANSAS BAPTIST COLLEGE.

In 1880, Arkansas Baptist College in Arkansas that Mason attended

He had spent many hours in searching the Scripture surrounding this second work of salvation. The Spirit of the Lord gave him many scriptural confirmations; assuring him that holy and righteous living was for the everyday Christian.[19]

In an 1893 summer-camp meeting in Preston, Arkansas, Charles Harrison Mason preached his first sermon surrounding his new faith of Holiness. Mason had rejected the Baptist doctrine of Calvinism many people know it as (Once Save Always Saved) that allowed individuals to live a sinful life while a Christian.[20] His took his first sermon text on Holiness from II Timothy 3:12–13, titled *Thou Therefore Endure Hardness as a Good Soldier of Jesus Christ.* The message stirred the congregation to want to know more about living a life of Holiness.[21] Wanting further confirmation he took a two-week sabbatical and completely sought God again. When he returned from the woods, he had new inspiration and dedicated his ministry concerning the doctrine of Holiness and Sanctification. Mason was conducting a revival at the same church he had spoken at, and he asked Mason if he would continue his revival. Mason would not give him an answer; he wanted to go by the Holy Spirit's instruction and said, "I felt that it was my first duty to consult the Lord. I went into the woods, fell on my knees and asked the Lord to show me evidence of my calling to the ministry of Holiness by giving me success in the sinners of his community being converting in this upcoming revival." [22] When Charles returned, back to the pastor's house, a religious woman cried out to me that she wanted to know the total salvation that he was preaching, and when the revival started back at church, many sinners came to Christ. The Lord had granted and restored Mason's ministry back to its rightful place from where he had fallen before his marriage to Alice. He saw God begin to work miracles of healing and deliverance with signs that followed his preaching ministry as he had read in the Bible in the New Testament about Jesus and his Apostles. Now he believed his calling was to draw many religious sinners to the Cross, converting them away from the assimilated doctrine of the white Baptist adopted by African

Americans to true biblical New Testament Holiness that Paul the Apostle had preached.[23]

END NOTES

Chapter 2: The Test of a Failed Marriage

1. James Courts, *The History and Life Work of Bishop C.H. Mason*, Privately Published: Memphis, TN, 1918, Page 20.

2. Burgess, Stanley M., and McGee, Gary B., *Dictionary of Pentecostal and Charismatic Movements*, Published by Zondervan, Grand Rapids, MI, 1988, Page 586.

3. James Courts, *The History and Life Work of Bishop C.H. Mason*, Privately Published: Memphis, TN, 1918, Page 20.

4. Ibid., Page 22

5. Ibid., Page

6. James Courts, *The History and Life Work of Bishop C.H. Mason*, Privately Published: Memphis, TN, 1918, Page 22.

7. Marriage Record of C.H. Mason and Alice Saxton, 1890, January, Faulkner County, Arkansas Family Ancestry Search individual record.

8. Louis F. Morgan, "The Flame Still Burns," *Charisma Christian Life Magazine*. Publisher Strang Publications, Issue November 2007, Page 44.

9. Elijah L. Hill, *Women Come Alive*, Arlington, Texas, P.O. Box 181937, (Independently Published), May, 2005, Page 64.

10. Ibid., Page 65

11. Ibid., Page 65

12. Ibid., Page 62

13. James Courts, *The History and Life Work of Bishop C.H. Mason*, Privately Published: Memphis, TN, 1918, Page 22.

14. Ibid., Page 22

15. Ibid., Page 22

16. Ibid., Page 23

17. Burgess, Stanley M., and McGee, Gary B., *Dictionary of Pentecostal and Charismatic Movements*, Published by Zondervan, Grand Rapids, MI, 1988, Page 586.

18. Bishop Ithiel C. Clemmons, *Bishop C.H. Mason and the roots of the Church of God in Christ,* Publisher: Pneuma Life Publishing, Bakersfield, California, 93389, Page 9.

19. Burgess, Stanley M., and McGee, Gary B., *Dictionary of Pentecostal and Charismatic Movements*, Published by Zondervan, Grand Rapids, MI, 1988, Page 586.

20. Dr. David Daniels. III, "The Theological Legacy of Bishop Charles Harrison Mason." *The Whole Truth Magazine*. Published By The Church of God in Christ Publishing Board, Memphis, TN, 2005, Page 30.

21. Louis F. Morgan, "The Flame Still Burns," *Charisma Christian Life Magazine*. Publisher Strang Publications, Issue November 2007, Page 44.

22. James Courts, *The History and Life Work of Bishop C.H. Mason*, Privately Published: Memphis, TN, 191, Page 24.
23. Ibid., Page 24.

Chapter 3—Rejecting a Lie for the Truth

It was November 1, 1893, when twenty-seven year old Rev. Charles Mason enrolled in the Arkansas Baptist College; to better prepare himself for his ministry.[1] Mason soon after within the first six months came to the conclusion school could not assist him in his preparation to help him in achieve his lifelong task of preserving slave religion. He believed that the effectual fervent prayers he had witnessed from the older slaves as a boy, was an important spiritual life style that God had given to African Americans.[2] Three months after Charles had enrolled in the college, he heard a lecture by Dr. Charles Lewis: who was Academic Dean of the college. Dr. Lewis was one of the top graduates of Morgan Park Seminary (Now the University of Chicago Divinity School.) In Ithiel Clemmons' book it stated, "He exposed hermeneutical & cultural discrepancies, which made Mason suspicious of the methods, philosophies, and curriculum at Arkansas Baptist College."[3]

It was not long before Mason concluded that the school could not assist him in preserving black slave religion. He discovered through Dr. Lewis' lecture, that the African Americans goal at this college was to assimilate into white Baptist religion, as a tradeoff for being accepted into America's mainstream culture.[4] He was appalled that many mainline black denominations in his day adopted a white denominations doctrines without taking the time to research those biblical truths for themselves scripturally.[5]

For some doctrines he believed were diluted with racism and a Eurocentric spin. Mason wanted nothing to do with their methods, philosophies, or curriculum; inevitably, white men tried to stir African Americans away from their true spiritual treasure; which he had found through praying with the older slaves and righteous living. Ithiel Clemmons wrote of Bishop Mason's true feelings surrounding this issue, "Mason also held suspect the *bourgeois* nature of many black churches. He had cultural, scriptural, and hermeneutical suspicions about the black church's emulation of white, reason-centered culture and religion."[6]

Therefore, Mason left the college, disheartened about their form of education and assimilated church methodology, for it contradicted what God was calling him to practice in his daily Christian walk with God.[7] He took on the challenge to seek out his doctrine with a line-by-line biblical foundational teaching style. He began to promote direct biblical theology exposed directly from biblical scriptures as he preached to the people. In addition, he loved the spiritual vitality and expressiveness that African Americans displayed openly before God as a true form of worship that the Father was seeking for such to worship him, and that the Holy Spirit was calling all human beings of all races to worship him in spirit and in true.

Charles Mason had witnessed a supernatural rich spiritual heritage he discovered in slave religion. This brought about his personal experience of his belief in divine healing, of which it had manifested in his personal life when God raising him up from the death.[8] He was not about to deny his past experience of fervent prayer and supernatural healing that he had learned from the older slaves. Their experience of prayer and fervent intercession with God had produced life-changing results. He did not want to exchange for a form of godliness that denied the power of God's miracle working power in the New Testament that he believed was still for God's people today. He could not understand why African Americans wanted to trade this rich experience of slave religion to be like Euro-American Baptist denomination to be like them just to receive social and cultural acceptance.[9] Mason felt they risked losing the power of this deeper chasing after God prayer experience, which was spiritually transferred to them from their ancestors. Mason wanted to restore the spirituality exhibited by blacks, like holy dances, ecstatic worship, and falling out under the power of the Holy Spirit.[10] It is during this period of enlightenment, that he met Charles Price Jones at Arkansas Baptist College. They were about the same age and quickly became friends and ministerial comrades.

In 1949, the cornerstone of St. Paul Church of God in Christ the mother church of the COGIC that Bishop Charles Harrison Mason founded in 1897 in Lexington, MS. Pastor O. S. Sheard was appointed the pastor who is Bishop John Henry Sheard's father Chairman of the Board of Bishops of the Church of God in Christ Worldwide, and General Board member Bishop Drew Sheard's grandfather.

Mason really admired C.P. Jones who gained the respect of the senior men of the Arkansas Baptist Convention. In 1884, at the age of nineteen, Charles Price conversion to Christ took place in the Baptist faith. He began to serve in his local church as a Sunday school teacher, and later that same year, accepted his call as a lay preacher.[11]

Elias Morris, the president of the Arkansas Baptist State Convention, realized the potential in C.P. Jones and encouraged him to not just preach, but also pursue his education to better prepare for ministry. C. P. Jones looked up to Elias Morris as his mentor and heeded his advice. In 1888, Charles Price enrolled in the Arkansas Baptist College to study for the ministry and sharpen his skills as a preacher of the Gospel of Jesus Christ. During this time, Jones became a popular young preacher, singer, and evangelist and found great favor with the denominational leaders. Strong black leaders like Charles Fisher and William Bacote of Marion, Alabama, became close companions of Jones.[12] He was ordained by Fisher at Mt. Zion Baptist Church, Little Rock, Arkansas. While attending the college, he became pastor of several prominent churches like People Creek Baptist Church and the St. Paul Baptist Church in the Arkansas area.

However, it was while he pastored the Bethlehem Baptist Church at Searcy, Arkansas, that he became editor of the main publication of the Baptist faith, the famous *Arkansas Baptist Vanguard Newspaper*.[13] His remarkable gifts and talents play the piano, write gospel music and preach attracted the attention of denominational leaders, and they elected him later as the secretary of the Arkansas Baptist State Convention. Historically, there were few who had become elevated so fast in the Baptist denomination as Charles Price Jones as an up and coming young preacher.

Both Mason and Jones got together at the Arkansas Baptist College and held strong convictions that the Baptist faith was not teaching the entire truth of the work of salvation. Therefore, people were living their lives ignorant to the fact that God required righteous living. Instead, they believed in the Baptist faith that it was okay to live any way they wanted to and still be a Christian.

In 1880, Elias Morris, President of the Arkansas Baptist Convention who expelled C.H. Mason and C.P. Jones

These two young preachers agreed to make known the truth of sanctification within the Baptist faith, and to expose the lie surrounding peoples' lack of experiencing the entire truth of the work of salvation that Christ purchased by his blood. [14] Mason's dynamic preaching, and Jones' prolific writing, preaching, and song-writing ability gave them the right equipment to influence the Baptist community in the South. As he spoke, Mason's words hit like a hammer, causing many to turn to the faith of holiness.[15] Even as a youth, he realized that it took self-sacrifice to know God's heart in a greater way. Jones recognized that there was a need to crucify the flesh in order for the Holiness principle (the second definitive work of salvation) to impact the believer's life. These two began to form a holiness group to study the Bible and seek God through fervent prayer and fasting. The following is an example the newspaper they started and published called, *The Truth,* April 1906:

> "Come, dear brethren, and let us lift up Christ together. Bring your Bibles. Come fasting and praying that we may have the same mind and mind the same things."[16]

Mason was willing to lay down all of his ministerial advancements and place God's will over the will of the great religious men of his day. Jones realized God had given him favor before the great senior men of the Baptist faith. What mattered even more to him was that he wanted to be, as Abraham, a friend of God.[16] C.P. Jones felt that the main leaders of the Baptist faith were "toying with Jesus," and did not proclaim the true Gospel of Christ to the people. He believed their doctrinal belief left the people in ignorance causing them to live beneath their spiritual privilege. [17]

In 1894, during the time when Jones was the pastor of the Tabernacle Baptist Church in Selma, Alabama, he was adamant about sharing his thoughts and convictions before his congregation and others, he finally preached from a Baptist pulpit the second definitive work of salvation. Eventually, he crossed paths with two other Baptist preachers that shared his same passion to seek God's truth. Their belief was they would seek instead of conforming to false teaching of their Baptist faith. J.E. Jeter, and W.S. Pleasant spent much time with Jones in prayer and fasting, while reflecting on the Scriptures that were relevant to sanctification, i.e., a second work of grace. [18]

In 1895, Jones and Mason released a bi-monthly periodical called *The Truth*, and because C.P. was one of the editors of the *Baptist Vanguard*, he had access to their mailing list. Jones, Mason and their comrades Jeter and Pleasant, began a campaign to spread the good news of holiness among all black Baptists in the south. [19]

At the Baptist Convention of 1896, Jones was to be the host pastor of the National Baptist Convention. In addition to Jones producing the *The Truth* publication, he also released a booklet called *A Treatise on I Corinthians 12: The Work of the Holy Spirit in the Church.* It was at this convention that Jones delivered a powerful message surrounding holiness to the Arkansas State Convention generating a profound effect upon the convention attendees. He preached with such power and conviction that the men in the convention sobbed, wept and cried out, "Stop him, Stop him."[20]

In a book written by Bishop Ithiel Clemmons, he states how Jones strictly adhered to Matthew 5:48, *"'Be ye therefore perfect, even as your Father which is in heaven is perfect.'"* Many Baptist congregants entered a new covenant with God striving towards godly perfection. Jones' motto for those living the higher Christian life was Christ All In All, No More I, But Christ.[21]

Bishop Clemmons also quoted Jones as saying, "Our movement was entirely interdenominational and in spirit anti-sectarian. The sick were healed, blind were made to see and the afflicted were blessed. Black and white, Jew and gentile sought God together." This is also the beginning of not just African Americans following Jones and Mason's Holiness movement but white brothers and sister joined and became a part of their newly formed churches in the South.

In 1885, Mason's First Revival in the old Gin house Lexington, MS

This the first church Mason founded 1895 in Lexington, MS after its new construction

The Holiness faith C.P. Jones and Charles Mason were expounding upon started an unquenchable fire. In addition, between 1896 and 1897, these pioneering preachers conducted revivals and camp meetings that influenced the growth of the Holiness Movement in the Southern states of Arkansas, Tennessee and Mississippi. Many blacks, from traditional Baptist and Methodist congregations, accepted this new way of holiness. Jones and Mason established Church of God congregations in Jackson, Lexington, and Natchez, Mississippi as well as in Little Rock, Arkansas, successfully spreading and establishing the Holiness Faith in the South.

Something unexpected occurred once while traveling in a wagon through Conway, Arkansas in 1894 directly after Jones and Mason left the Arkansas Baptist College to begin the Holiness faith on their own. A crowd began to surround them as Jones played the piano and Mason preached; but what was unusual about this crowd was that it contained whites as well as blacks. Moreover, Mason just started preaching what God gave him to preach. People of both races were on the housetops and in the fields listening. The Holy Spirit had drawn them there.[22] The crowd got so large that one of the town police officers came over to Mason and told him he would have to shut it down. Mason believed the police officer told him this because so many white people were attracted to the power of the gospel that he preached. Nevertheless, the officer broke up the crowd; but a white brother came up to Mason and told him, "We don't want you to stop preaching around here. The white preachers take up a collection why do not you start a church. I have some money here and some of my friends are with me. Let's go back in the woods and build a church." Mason would later state remembering this history that in 1950 that this white brother is still a part of his ministry in an audio recording. He also pointed out that he knew his mother and that his whole family faithfully supported of Mason's ministry for over the past fifty years.

Before and during Plessy vs. Ferguson between 1893-1960's many Pentecostal groups joined the Church of God in Christ as a religious fellowship carrying their name

In 1945, Bishop Charles Harrison Mason Fellowshipping with Whites

In the audio recording Mason asked several members of their family to stand up before the assembly as a testimony to his ministry to gather white and blacks together as God's people through the gospel of Jesus Christ`.[23]

This pattern of interracial mixing in religious worship services took place within Mason's ministry from 1894-1961 unto his death within the Church of God in Christ. At the beginning of Mason's Holiness movement through the gospel of Jesus Christ, Mason contradicted through his religious services America's jurisprudence of Plessy vs. Ferguson of 1896 that established segregation in America. This began to take place twelve years prior to Mason experiencing the in filling of the Holy Spirit in Los Angeles, California in 1907 under William J. Seymour's ministry at the Azusa Street Missions Revival. When Mason later experienced the infilling, and saw also the intermixing of races white and black worshiping together at Azusa this only confirmation to him that God was calling for him gather blacks and whites together to worship God despite Jim Crow laws in America.

In 1897, the revival fires fell in Lexington, Mississippi. Elder Mason delivered his first sermon at the south entrance of the courthouse. The next night, a Mr. John Lee invited Elder Mason to use his living room. Due to the overwhelming number that attended, a Mr. Watson, the owner of an old abandoned Gin house located on the bank of the creek nearby, he gave his consent to transfer the revival meeting there.[24]   People gathered all around the meeting area it cover the whole farming community. The people came from the surrounding communities to witness the healings and miracles that God manifested in Mason's ministry. Albeit, there were some members of the Baptist faith who were outraged and appalled at the success of this gathering that they fired five pistol shots, and two double barrel shotgun blasts into the crowd of attendees while the people were shouting and praying. Several people were shot that night, but thankfully, to their amazement none of the shots was fatal. The media hear about this incident and they published about this event in the local newspaper, which promoted and increased future attendance of the meeting. This caused others to believe more that this Holiness Movement was of God.

Due to the success of the revival, the old gin house became too small. It was not long before until the seating capacity was so overwhelming that a new edifice came under construction. Therefore, Mason and Jones purchased a lot and built an edifice, dedicating it to God. With the establishment of this Church of God were sixty charter members. The congregants voted that Charles Mason should become the pastor. He conducted his first baptismal service on the first Sunday of March 1897. There were three individuals baptized: Addie Golden, Lulu McCullough and Charles Pleas, Jr.[24]

From the seventeenth to the nineteenth century, most blacks had experienced Christianity at the influence of these two organizations: the Baptist and the Methodist churches. Mason and Jones had created a phenomenal change in the landscape of the southern religious experience by establishing a black denomination, which had no assimilation doctrinally by white, America.[25] They believed in a second definitive work of grace, the doctrine of holiness, and they adapted *this* doctrine for the new organization. A new black denomination had started in the South that did not assimilate their religious practices and doctrines from white similar religious institutions. Subsequently, Mason, Jones and their colleagues because of the spread of their new faith received opposition by the leaders of the Baptist faith.

This new experience spread throughout the states of Mississippi, Arkansas and Tennessee. The National Baptist Convention decided to expel Mason, Jones and their colleagues from the Baptist faith officially. The convention explained the reasons for their expulsion, saying, "C.P. Jones, W.J. Pleasant and C.H. Mason were preaching pernicious, heretical doctrines among the *"most ignorant classes of our people, leading off individuals and corrupting churches."* The expelling took place on July 23, 1899, C.P. Jones, C.H. Mason and all of their followers after President E.C. Morris gave his presidential address at the convention. President E. C. Morris, who was a big supporter of both of these young men in the past and had encouraged them to resume college, but reluctantly excommunicate them from his Baptist organization's fellowship.[26]

Some seven years later C.H. Mason prayerfully sought the Lord on a name that would distinguish them from other existing denominations, and the Holy Spirit revealed to him the name *Church of God in Christ*. The Lord revealed the Scripture to him to support his revelation it was found in I Thessalonians 2:14, which states, *"For ye, brethren, became followers of the churches of God which in Judaea are in Christ Jesus...."* Later, they renamed the organization and all of the brethren unanimously agreed to the name *Church of God in Christ* for their Holiness organization. The General body of believer chose Elder C. P. Jones as the General overseer of the organization, and Elder Charles Harrison Mason overseer of Tennessee and Elder Jeter as overseer of Arkansas. They made an application of incorporation to the Clergy Bureau in Washington, D.C., who accepted the name *Church of God in Christ*. The name of the official corporation, and the new denomination started as The Church of God In Christ (COGIC).

Here is the following introductory statement made by C.P. Jones at the calling of the winter convention of 1906, in Jackson, Mississippi, that demonstrated their adoption of the name Church of God in Christ name:

> "To the Church of God in Christ: greetings. In the fear of God, and as we pray and hope, in the Spirit and mind of Christ, as president of the Convocation of the Church of God in Christ, it is necessary that I now have printed in book form, those rules adopted among us and to church government agreeing with the pattern of the New Testament as the Lord made us see it and agree to it in Elders Council assembled."[27]

The Triumph of the Black Church

In 1940, Pastor James Delk beaten by the Klu Klux Klan because him being white in an African American religious organization, and he ran for Governor of Kentucky on a platform that white people should treat black folks better.

In 1907, D. J. Young was one of the three that attended Azusa with Mason, and Young was appointed the first Editor of the Church of God in Christ Whole Truth Paper

In 1910, E. R. Driver   In 1951, Dr. Arenia C. Mallory

In 1963, World Headquarters Executive Board

There were times that Charles Mason suffered great persecution at the hands of those that did not like the Holiness Doctrine he so adamantly preached. He would never let these hardships deter him from continuing his preaching campaigns. His crusades reached out to many other races, including whites that had to come see what kind of man this was that affected many for Christ.

The white brother who earlier supported Elder Mason's ministry was James Delk. He was beaten twice by the Ku Klux Klan (a diabolical, white southern-resistance group, whose origins were around the end of the Civil War) for being a white man that followed the ministry of a black man Charles Harrison Mason.[28] This did not dissuade James from continuing his faithful support, and he would later become one of the elders under Mason's leadership for over thirty years until his death. Elder Delk's service was a tremendously positive impact for the ministry. James Delk stated that, he witnessed the white president of the railroad company convert to Holiness at one of Mason's Revivals.[29] And God even gave Elder Mason favor with the railroad, insomuch that the president would allow Mason and other ministers licensed under his organization to receive a discount for riding on the train. Mason's preaching had broken the color line in the Deep South and caused white as well as black to come into fellowship under the banner of Holiness. Delk remembered how Mason would walk from town to town, through the cotton fields of Mississippi and Arkansas, preaching outdoors in the open air. When farm workers heard that Mason was coming it was as if a holiday people would gather from different counties from three to four thousand would come to attend his revival services. The crowds gathered to hear this charismatic preacher and wanted him to lay his hands on them for healing.

Elder Delk (who would later become the founder and pastor of a Church of God in Christ in Madisonville, Kentucky) made some profound statements regarding his following the ministry of an African American leader during climate of Jim Crow in America:

"I doubt if there has ever been a minister who has lived since the day of the Apostles, who has shown the sweet spirit to all people, regardless of race, creed or color, or has preached with greater power than Brother Mason. I have met and heard William Booth, the founder of the Salvation Army; Brother Brazil, founder of the Nazarene Church; Brother Bell, founder of the Assembly of God; and Rev. Thomlison of the Church of God. I have also heard D.L. Moody preach and was personally acquainted with Rev. Paul Reader and both Aimee Semple McPherson and the late Billy Sunday for thirty years, but of all of the great preachers I have read after and met personally, no one has that sweetness and meekness of Jesus like that of our Senior Bishop, C.H. Mason."[30]

"Not long ago. I was talking to a white friend of mine, who had heard me preach several times, and he said to me, "I love a negro in his place." Then I quickly asked him, "Do you love a white man out of his place?" And he replied "No sir." We say that America believes in free speech, free schools and free press, and I am giving you some of it at this time. We white people have been 400 years getting to where we are, and bear in mind at the close of the Civil War 80 years ago, the negroes in the South had scarcely a second shirt to their backs, and did not know a from z. All of this was due to the fact that they were in slavery. During the 80 years which have followed the Civil War, the Negro race has come from ignorance to intelligence, from poverty to prosperity and to civilization more rapidly than any race in the world."

In 1905, Mason married his second wife Lelia W. Mason most of his children were from this marriage

In the early 1940's after Lelia Mason's death Bishop Mason married, Elsie Mason seated L-R Elsie Mason, Bishop C.H. Mason, Standing L-R, Bishop J.O. Patterson, and Bishop L.H. Ford

"Among the Negro race, we have as fine statesmen, educators and religious leaders as we have among any nationality of people in America. They are progressive and it is a shame in my judgment for the southern white people to call them the slang word "Nigger," that forces them to call white people "White Trash." Both statements are wrong. Whenever we get Jesus in our hearts, nick-naming people and hating people, segregation and Jim Crow vanish away like the smoke of the hour."[31]

And after being single for thirteen years and totally focusing on his ministry, Mason married Lelia Washington on October 18, 1905. The marriage license listed as a witness, Bishop Mason's friend and church member, Deacon William Roberts. William Roberts would play a very significant role in Bishop Charles H. Mason's national ministry in later years by pioneering the Church of God in Christ in the Chicago, Illinois area. Mason's best friend in ministry, Elder C.P. Jones, performed his marriage to Lelia Washington.[32]

END NOTES

Chapter 3: Rejecting a Lie for the Truth

1. Bishop Ithiel C. Clemmons, *Bishop C.H. Mason and the roots of the Church of God in Christ*, Publisher: Pneuma Life Publishing, Bakersfield, California, 93389, Page 7
2. C. F. Range Editor, *Church of God In Christ Official Manuel*, Publisher Church of God In Christ Publishing Board. 1973, Page XXIV.
3. Burgess, Stanley M., and McGee, Gary B., *Dictionary of Pentecostal and Charismatic Movements,* Published by Zondervan, Grand Rapids, MI, 1988, Page 586.
4. Ibid., Page 586.
5. Ibid., Page 586.
6. Bishop Ithiel C. Clemmons, *Bishop C.H. Mason and the Roots of the Church of God in Christ,* Publisher: Pneuma Life Publishing, Bakersfield, California, 93389, Page 18.
7. Ibid., Page 6.
8. Ibid., Page 6
9. Ibid., Page 6
10. Louis F. Morgan, "The Flame Still Burns," *Charisma Christian Life Magazine*. Publisher Strang Publications, Issue November 2007, Page 44.
11. Otho Cobbins, *History of Church of Christ (Holiness) U.S.A.,* 1895-1965 (New York: Vantage Press, 1965), 428-429.
12. Bishop Ithiel C. Clemmons, *Bishop C.H. Mason and the Roots of the Church of God in Christ,"* Publisher: Pneuma Life Publishing, Bakersfield, California, 93389, Page 8.
13. J.H. Green's Introduction to C.P. Jones, *Appeal to The Sons of Africa*, Jackson, MS: Truth, 1902.
14. Charles H. Pleas, *Fifty Years of Achievement: Church of God in Christ"* Privately Published: Kansas City, KS, 1955, Page 1
15. Bishop Ithiel C. Clemmons, *"Bishop C.H. Mason and the Roots of the Church of God in Christ,* Publisher: Pneuma Life Publishing, Bakersfield, California, 93389, Page 17.
16. *The Truth*, religious periodical, April 1906, published by C.P. Jones, in Jackson, Tennessee.
17. Charles H. Pleas, *Fifty Years of Achievement: Church of God in Christ* Privately Published: Kansas City, KS, 1955, Page 1
18. Ibid., Page 1
19. James Courts, *The History and Life Work of Bishop C.H. Mason*, Privately Published: Memphis, TN, 1919, Page 25.

20. Bishop Ithiel C. Clemmons, *Bishop C.H. Mason and the Roots of the Church of God in Christ*, Publisher: Pneuma Life Publishing, Bakersfield, California, 93389, Page 7.
21. J.H. Green's Introduction to C.P. Jones, "Appeal to the Sons of Africa", Jackson, MS: *Truth*, 1902.
22. Bishop Ithiel C. Clemmons, *Bishop C.H. Mason and the roots of the Church of God in Christ*, Publisher: Pneuma Life Publishing, Bakersfield, California, 93389, Page 13.
23. Elijah L. Hill. (Copyright 2012). Title DVD Recording *Follow Peace with All Men*. Reproduction of Audio on DVD, Arlington, Texas. Original date of this audio recording was 1950 Bishop Charles Harrison Mason's personal sermon. Memphis, TN.
24. Charles H. Pleas, *Fifty Years of Achievement: Church of God in Christ*, Privately Published: Kansas City, KS, 1955, Page 4, 5.
25. Charles H. Pleas, *Fifty Years of Achievement: Church of God in Christ,* Privately Published: Kansas City, KS, 1955, Page 5.
26. Vinson Synan, *The Holiness-Pentecostal Movement in the U.S.* (Grand Rapids, MI: William B. Eerdmans, 1971).
27. E.C. Morris, *Sermons, Addresses, Reminiscences and Important Correspondence*, 1901 (Reprint. New York: Arno Press, 1980).
28. *Rules of Government of the Churches of God in Christ*, printed in the winter catalogue for the Winter Convention, part of the evidence entered in the case, Frank Avant vs. C.H. Mason, January 14-21, 1906.
29. James Delk, *He Made Millions Happy* (Hopkinsville, KY: Privately Published, 1950).
30. Ibid., Page 7
31. James L. Delk, *Philosophy and Democracy*, Hopkinsville, KY: Privately Published, 1945, Page 9, 10.
32. Marriage Record of C.H. Mason and Lelia Washington, Memphis, Shelby County, Tennessee, October 18, 1905, roll #113.

Chapter 4—Enlightenment and Betrayal

Bishop Charles Harrison Mason establishing doctrine for the institution of Modern Day Holiness/Pentecost, and he, along with C.P. Jones, instituted this new Holiness denomination in 1897 (ten years prior to Pastor Seymour of the Azusa Street Revivals of 1906). Mason had evolved from the Baptist faith, converting to the explosive Holiness Doctrine that swept across the southern United States. He and Jones catapulted to notoriety through conventions, revivals, and periodicals. Thousands of converts accepted this uncompromising holy standard of living. This shook the very foundation of the Baptist and Methodist faith, which caused many to want more than just *a religion.*[1]

The favor of God was upon Mason as he established several churches through his administrative and organizational gift; launching a large network of holiness churches under the Church of God in Christ banner from 1894-1907. However, in spite of everything God was doing in his life, Mason knew something was still missing. He withdrew in earnest and fervent prayer: hungering and thirsting after God in an even greater way. And God used C.P. Jones to help open his eyes through the Holy Scriptures in Acts 2:1-4 which speaks of the infilling of the Holy Ghost on the Day of Pentecost. C.P. Jones scripturally convinced Elder Mason that they were missing the experience of the Holy Ghost according to Matthew 10:8. This verse shows clearly that we might have power to heal the sick, cast out devils and to raise the dead, yet not have the evidence of speaking in tongues."[2] As a result, Mason along with two of his comrades, traveled to the Azusa Street out-pouring in 1907: to personally witness this new Holy Ghost infilling experience. They wanted to know for themselves if this truly was an actual move of God's Spirit in the earth.

In 1907, C.H. Mason, D.J. Young, and Jeter attend the Azusa Street Mission and receive the Baptist of the Holy Spirit

In 1906, here is a picture of the saints at the Azusa Street Mission, with Pastor Seymour sitting in the middle.

After Mason arrived there attending the Azusa Street Mission services, he discovered that it was indeed of God; and he humbled himself and fell on his face to seek God to receive the Pentecostal experience for himself as he witnessed for himself others speaking in tongues as they received the Baptism of the Holy Spirit. At the revival in Los Angeles, California, Mason saw it with his own eyes the sick healed; people spoke in another language and sang in tongues. Seeing these observations placed in him a hunger that was deeper than anything he had ever felt before. Undeniably, this New Testament experience was real and Mason wanted this Holy Ghost infilling for himself.[5] At the conclusion of Mason, Jeter and Young's five-week stay at Azusa Street Mission, these three ministers from Tennessee finally received the baptism of the Holy Spirit. The February-March issue of Pastor Seymour's *Apostolic Faith Periodical* noted it: "March 19th was a wonderful day at the Mission on Azusa St. Three ministers from Tennessee received the endowment of power from on High and the glory of God filled the upper room. Others received the anointing of the Sprint and some were slain under the power of God."[6]

Mason amazed to see that whites, blacks and Hispanics worshipped under Pastor Seymour's ministry also. He had only seen this mixture of races within his ministry in the Church of God in Christ Holiness from the time his first revival started in 1894 in Conway, Arkansas. Though he had many dedicated white men within his ministry, this multicultural worship experience was a remarkable sight. This would be his final confirmation that it was God's will for him to gather all people of all races and creeds to worship God under the power of the Gospel of Jesus Christ. All of this was taking place during America's Jim Crow laws fifty years prior to the civil rights movement. Isn't it interesting that the late Dr. Martin Luther King Jr., stated sixty years later, "The most segregated time in American is on Sunday morning when we all go to our several houses of worship based upon our color."

In 1906, at Azusa Street Mission, Los Angeles, CA, L-R, standing, Brother Adams, F.F. Bosworth, and Tom Hezmalhalch, Seated L-R, William J. Seymour, and John Lake.

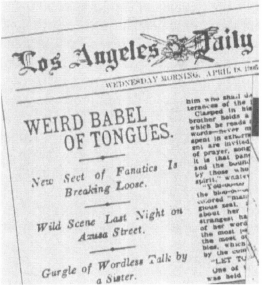

1906, Los Angeles Daily Reports on Mission

Yet, Mason's ministry would contradict Dr. Martin Luther King's statement by experiencing multicultural worship from 1894 when he left the Arkansas Baptist College holding his first out door meeting when whites and blacks gather to hear him preach, while C.P. Jones played the piano. In an audio tape recording in the 1950's Mason confirms himself how his ministry starred from Conway, Arkansas was multicultural, and that God manifested this miracle of the interracial interaction within his ministry, and Mason stated, "God had given him the ministry to Gather together my people of all races white and black." The mandate that Bishop Charles Harrison Mason took upon himself was God's will prophetically challenging America's jurisprudence of Plessy vs. Ferguson of 1896, which was man's will to segregate the white and black races in America.

The theological position of William Seymour was to love your neighbor as yourself, the second greatest commandment given by our Lord and Savior Jesus Christ. He believed in a Christianity that was divorced of racial segregation and embraced an interracial worship experience. The tragic error of mainline denominations was that African Americans took their doctrine from their white counterparts. One main example of this erroneous doctrine is that white Christians used Christianity to justify slavery teaching that African Americans were descendants of Ham, and were therefore cursed to be the slaves (see Gen. 9:25). However, Pastor Seymour and Bishop Mason separated themselves from this misinterpretation and misrepresentation of Scripture and developed the true doctrinal position of interracial worship from God rather than man's revelation of the Holy Scriptures.[7] William Seymour's stance on theological teaching and preaching of interracial unity is the manifestation of love from God through Holy living. One thing that white scholars left out of history was written on the side of the Azusa Street Mission (Bishop Seymour's ministry theme): " Whosoever Shall Enter Here, Let Brotherly Love Continue." Love for one another, regardless of color, is the true manifestation of the Holy Spirit's presence in the life of the believer.[8]

All of these things continued to have a profound impact on Bishop C.H. Mason. For, since his arrival in Los Angeles, he marveled at the doctrinal teaching of Pastor William J. Seymour surrounding women in ministry, interracial worship and divine love as the manifestation of the Holy Spirit Baptism. Mason stated in his personal observation of Elder Seymour's appeal and doxology (that consisted of a three-point appeal at the conclusion of his sermon), "All of those that want to be sanctified or baptized with the Holy Ghost, go to the upper room, and those that want to be healed go to the prayer room, and those that want to be justified, come to the alter."[11] Mason stated that his words were sweet and powerful; he later wrote, "Just as I attempted to bow down, someone called me and told me the pastor wants you three brethren in his room, I obeyed and went up.[12] Then Pastor William Seymour stated, "Brethren, the Lord will do great things for us and bless us." He cautioned us not to be running around in the city seeking worldly pleasure, but to seek pleasure of the Lord.[13]

The second night of service at the Azusa Street Mission, Bishop Mason saw a vision as God's presence filled the room. He stated, "I saw myself standing alone and had a dry roll of paper. I had to chew it. When I had gotten it all in my mouth trying to swallow it, looking up toward the heavens there appeared a man at my side. I turned my eyes at once: then I awoke and the interpretation came. God had me swallowing the whole book, and that if I did not turn my eyes to anyone but God and Him only, He would baptize me."[14] This vision revealed to him how he would carry the Pentecostal doctrine, and the manifestation of interracial worship of Pastor Seymour to the world, through his Church of God in Christ organization. Mason indeed became one of the most influential leaders in the infancy stage of the Modern Day Pentecostal Movement. To confirm this point, almost twelve years later, Pastor William J. Seymour would visit Bishop Mason at his world headquarters during his 12th Holy Convocation in Memphis, Tennessee, in December 10, 1919.[5]

MINUTES OF THE 12TH GENERAL CONVOCATION
Memphis, Tennessee
December 10, 1919

Twelfth Annual Session of the General Board of Elders was called to order at 10 o'clock by Dr. E.R. Driver of ... California. Song by Elder J.E. Bryant of Temple, Texas styled: "There Is No Condemnation." Pastor ... son of Omaha, Nebraska read for a lesson James, 4th chapter. Prayer by all, led by Pastor W.O. Der ... oke, Virginia. Dr. Driver was then offered to the body for chairman by Pastor G.E. Smith of Austin, Texas ... was re-elected by the body. Eld. J.E. Bryant was then offered to the body for secretary by Dr. Driver and ... d by the body.

... chairman then in his calm and pleasant manner made a few opening remarks in which our hearts rejoiced ... ished us as being great men because God had made us great. He then gave a most beautiful outline of the ... that demanded our consideration and announced the house in order for business. First in order we ... for Pastor F.W. Winda of Lexington, MS, suggested that each overseer make out his roll and turn it o ... D.J. Young of Kansas City for publication. Carried Elder R.R. Booker of St. Louis MO asked concern ... of Evangelist. A suggestion offered by Dr. R.E. Hart of Jackson, TN that the evangelist must be subject ...

In 1919, December these minutes records William J. Seymour's
Visit to the Church of God in Christ acknowledging Bishop Mason
For contending for his original faith of interracial worship

In 1922 on September William J. Seymour dies

This event occurred three years before Pastor William Seymour's death when he died in March 1922. The special visit he made was to acknowledge and place his blessing upon the importance of the Church of God in Christ movement within the future of Modern Day Pentecost. The recording secretary in the assembly of a thousand or more pastors and overseers throughout the United States, which followed the ministry of Bishop Charles Harrison Mason; dated Thursday, December 10, 1919 the minutes stated:

> "Elder W.J. Seymour of Chicago, who also was one of the founders of this great movement, came to us at this hour. How glad our hearts were made to meet him. Order of business was suspended for a few minutes to greet him. Elder Seymour then spoke of his long and wearisome trip and how glad he was to get here. He said he looked upon the Church of God in Christ to be the greatest movement on earth. Therefore, he rejoiced to stand among the greatest people on earth. He asked us to contend for the doctrine. He also repudiated even the thought of fornication in the ministry. In his conclusion, he urged that the ministry not only be fruitful but to show their fruits. Chief Apostle Mason made some very timely remarks by way of responding in the noble sayings of Elder Seymour. He concluded by singing in the spirit a song of welcome."[16]

Bishop Mason, as well as Pastor Seymour, taught that a tongue without the practice of breaking down barriers of malice, hatred and prejudice was not true Christianity. Their theological perspectives took on an eschatological message that for God's Bride the prejudice of American culture had no place in God's kingdom business. The Apostle John saw in heaven in the book of Revelations 7:9, John saw a number that no man could number of every race, tongue and creed worshipping God together this was

God's desire for his kingdom to be on earth as it is in heaven. In the prayer, that Jesus left the Body of Christ to pray in Matthews 6:10, which stated, "Thy Kingdom Come." Thy will be done in earth, as it is in Heaven." Jesus encouraged the Body of Christ to pray for God's Kingdom to come or his government to be made manifested in the earth realm as it is in Heaven. Our role as Pentecostals was to bring God's heavenly Democratization into the earth, which is God's government that is in conflict with man's government in the earth. William J. Seymour and Mason taught that the Pentecostal's were carving out a message of reconciliation of all God's children in order for the true government of the Kingdom of Heaven to materialize on this earth before Christ's return.[24] This was the true unadulterated doctrinal teaching of the Azusa Street Mission; the true original spiritual legacy of Pentecostalism in America and throughout the globe.

One of the Scriptures that penetrated Mason's denominational culture is Hebrews 12:14 it states, *"Follow peace with all men, and holiness, without which no man shall see the Lord."* This statement from the older saints in Pentecostalism meant that you had to live right in order for your Christian faith to have any real substance. This included the fact that true holiness meant to pursue peace with *all* men. For instance, Mason believed that an individual could not profess to have the Holy Ghost and be at odds with his brother pertaining to racist issues. How can one stand on the integrity of God's Word, and desire to harm one's sister or brother of another race? He believed that without that level of true Holiness no man would see the Lord. He believed in treating one another racially as equals on this earth, and that the gospel releases us from racial indifferences and racial inequalities.

In spite of the receiving the life-changing experience at the Azusa Street Mission, when Mason returned to Tennessee his trusted companion C.P. Jones rejected his glossolalia (speaking in tongues) experience. The leader of the Church of God in Christ Charles Price Jones, who ironically was the individual who convinced Mason and the others to go to Azusa to seek out the necessity of the Holy Spirit Baptism. He became resentful of

Mason having received the Holy Spirit Baptism before he did. His reasoning was that Mason might succeed him in becoming the chief Apostle of the Church of God in Christ movement. Elder Charles Mason was the most anointing speaker in their movement many churches were establish by his anointed ministry.[27] Therefore, C.P. Jones got together with Jeter, his longtime friend who had accompanied Mason to Azusa, and conspired to plant a seed amongst the brethren in the Church of God in Christ Holiness that Mason was teaching heresy against the Church of God in Christ faith. Jeter would be the eyewitness against Mason, since he had went to Azusa with him to testify before the Church of God in Christ Holiness Elder's Council.

While Mason was sharing with the people about his Azusa experience, he was completely unaware that two of his closest companions were conspiring against him. For C.P. Jones desired to maintain the supreme leadership of the fastest growing black denomination in the South.[28] And he refused to humble himself to experience the Holy Spirit baptism, even though he knew it was an experience for the modern day believer. Jones and Jeter put out lies about Mason that he was disillusioned and had lost his sanity by speaking in a new language. They told the people that his teachings about receiving the Holy Spirit baptism were against the Scripture.[29] This dissention eventually brought about two separate groups of theological thoughts within the Church of God in Christ: the tongue speakers and the no-tongue speakers.

Mason began to realize that his two companions were planting seeds of division amongst the people within his Church of God in Christ Holiness organization surrounding his preaching on the baptism of the Holy Ghost. Therefore, this issue was brought before the elders' council on August 29, 1907, for debate.[30] The elders stayed for three days and three nights, debating and searching the Bible to validate their positions. Mason's theological position obviously was a threat to Jones because he was the leader of this Holiness Movement, but he had not experienced the Baptism of the Holy Ghost with the initial evidence of speaking in tongues.

D.J. Young, C.H. Mason, R.R. Booker, E.M. Page, W.B. Holt, William Roberts, J.E. Bowe, N.T. Samuel, R.H.I. Clark, E.R. Driver, Charles Pleas, J.H. Boon, R.E. Hart

In 1910, the first overseers (Bishops) of the Church of God in Christ who started with Bishop Charles Harrison Mason when he started in 1907

In 1962, right after the death of Bishop Mason the executive board standing L-R, Bishop White, Bishop Shipman, Bishop Bennett, Bishop Crouch, Bishop Kelly, Bishop Bailey, Bishop Lyles, Bishop Wells, Bishop Brewer, Bishop Ford, seated L-R, Bishop McEwen, Senior Bishop O.T. Jones, Sr., Bishop J.O. Patterson

Therefore, Charles P. Jones as the chief Apostle of the Church of God in Christ Holiness instructed the General Assembly of the Elder's Council to excommunicate Mason from their new denomination, saying that his doctrine was heretical.

On September 4, 1907, Bishop Mason released this statement before his congregation after his excommunication from the denomination:

> "September 4, 1907. The General Assembly for the majority of members, having removed Elder C.H. Mason and those under him, put the matter square before the saints. He said: "We are preaching that Jesus' blood cleanses, His spirit sanctifies, and Jesus baptizes with the Holy Ghost." The preliminaries were to the extent that as in the years gone by, to not be cramped, but be frank in their conviction. And all stood save about five or six."[33]

Mason was shocked that C.P. Jones, his companion in ministry for ten years, whom he loved and admired, would go as far as putting him out of the very denomination that he helped to organize. Mason left the Assembly after their agreement to reject him from their fellowship, and almost half of the ministers left with Mason holding fast that Pentecost was for the believers' present-day experience.[34] Hurt by this move against him, Mason spent time in prayer to God to overcome the feeling of betrayal. He felt like David suffering his biggest wound from the one he served as his true friend, by the very one who went to the temple with him to pray. This was one of his worst pains, other than when his wife Alice Sexton divorced him because he wanted to preach the gospel. Now his best friend in ministry had betrayed and conspired against him falsely, in order to remove him from the picture as a possible future leader of the Church of God in Christ Movement.[35]

Mason called for a meeting by sending out letters to the brothers and sisters who believed as he did in the baptism in the Holy Ghost and the initial evidence of speaking in tongues. The meeting date was set for September of 1907, hosted in Memphis,

Tennessee. Two things took place: first, they elected Mason as their Chief Apostle and General Overseer, and second, their Pentecostal Church of God in Christ Holy Convocation was set to convene from November 25 to December 14, annually.[36] In November 1907, those that responded to Mason's call were: E.R. Diver, J. Bowe, R.R. Booker, R.E. Hart, W. Welsh, A.A. Blackwell, E. M. Page, R.H.I. Clark, D.J. Young, James Brewer, Daniel Spearman and J.H. Boone. The conference took place at 392 South Wellington Street, Memphis, Tennessee and they organized the first Pentecostal General Assembly of the Church of God in Christ. The Elder D. J. Young, who accompanied Mason to Azusa, became the editor of the Church of God in Christ Pentecostal *Whole Truth Newspaper*. The church of God in Christ Holiness' newspaper name was *The Truth*. However, Mason named his *The Whole Truth*, signifying the full gospel message of the New Testament Apostles that believed in receiving the Baptism of the Holy Ghost.

The three most educated individuals present at the 1907 meeting were Dr. E. R. Hart (attorney & law professor), Elder Eddie R. Driver (attorney), and David J. Young. They drafted a resolution to reinstate Mason under their newly organized convention. The following is the new newly formed Pentecostal Church of God in Christ statement drafted on Mason's behalf:

> "Whereas it is reported in *The Truth* that Elder C. H. Mason, dealt with by a convention called together in Jackson, Mississippi, on Thursday, August the 29th, 1907. The finding was the withdrawal of the right-hand of fellowship. And whereas, the Holiness Assembly of the Churches of God, did meet in the month of January 1906, and elected Elder C.H. Mason one of the chief pastors or overseers.
>
> And Whereas, the committee assigned no true reason from their heads and unconsidered action,

In 1934, The Old Tabernacle that burned down in 1936

In 1932, at Bishop Mason's church National Convocation

In 1948, World Headquarters, L-R, seated, Bishop Bryant, Bishop Mason, Mother Lillian Brooks-Coffey, Bishop Riley Williams

we the ministers of the Church of God, assembled in Memphis, this 4th day of September, 1907, do reaffirm his election as declared by the Tennessee Assembly of all the Churches of God, which met at Jackson, Mississippi, January 1906. All of which we respectfully submit. Signed by R.E. Hart, E.R. Driver, and D.J. Young."[37]

On January 8, 1908, one month after Bishop C.H. Mason had founded his own Pentecostal organization; C.P. Jones filed an injunction against him in the Shelby County Court ordering Mason to appear in court, alleging that he had to give up the use of his church property in Memphis, Tennessee. At Mason's church, a no-tongue speaking faction of his church membership disagreed with his teaching on receiving the baptism of the Holy Spirit. In addition, C.P. Jones and his elder's council joined Mason's church members in the suit that implemented an injunction against Mason to remove him from Pastor of their church.

C.P. Jones attempted to take control of all of Mason's church properties that he had established while in the Church of God in Christ Holiness. By implementing this lawsuit, C.P. Jones' goal was to strip Mason of all of his church properties. Three other groups came against Mason in this lawsuit, which included the Elder's Council of the Church of God in Christ Holiness, four members of the Saints' Home Church in Memphis, Tennessee, and a group of Baptist ministers that claimed Mason's teaching of tongues was disruptive to the black Christian community. The Honorable Judge Frederick Hugh Heiskell presided over the case, and Bishop Charles Mason employed the attorney H.R. Saddler to defend him in the civil case.[39]

Instead of dissolving the lawsuit against the defendants, Judge Heiskell ordered the court to allow depositions from both sides. The members of the Saints' Home Church in Memphis, TN that came as complainants against Mason were, Frank Avant, Henry Scott, Sidney Reaves and Robert Davis, who were the "no-tongue faction" that disagreed with Mason's new Holy Ghost baptism preaching. The Judge ruled in the favor of C.P. Jones and the members of Mason's church C.P. Jones had collaborated with to oust Mason from the church he had founded in 1897.[40] Bishop Mason realized they had concocted an ingenious plan against him after he lost the first court trial in local court in the state of Tennessee. Therefore, he changed attorney's and secured R.E. Hart one of the founding Overseer's within Mason's Pentecostal Church of God in Christ organization as his attorney. Dr. E. R. Hart noticed that Mason's trial was unfair immediately appealed the local Shelby County's Judges Decision to the appellate court of the state of Tennessee to reargue the loopholes in the lower courts argument and final decision.[41]

Dr. E. R. Hart was a prominent pastor in the CME church who had received the Holy Spirit under Bishop Mason. He was one of the founding members who organized the COGIC in 1907. He became the first Overseer of Tennessee appointed by Bishop Mason. Dr. Hart had a unique background. He had co-founded the University of Tennessee and received his medical and law degree from there, and he was the second African American to obtain this medical license in the State of Tennessee. Dr. Hart was able to identify three violations in the local Judges ruling, on Mason's behalf in 1909.[42]

Under Dr. Hart's cross-examination, the local judge's decision did not stand up to the higher Appellate Court's decision. As a result of this higher court's judicial decision it reversed the local Shelby County Court decision, and gave Mason back access to his church in Memphis, Tennessee. This final legal action gave Bishop Mason's organization the right to take possession of Saints' Home Church of God in Christ in Memphis, Tennessee, and forced C.P. Jone's organization to reorganize under a new name called the Church of Christ Holiness (USA).[43]

In 1910, Leonard P Adams was the first to form a white fellowship of churches under Bishop Mason, he testified on Mason's behalf at his trial in 1908. Pastor Adams was the first overseer of Bishop Mason headquarters jurisdiction from 1910-1918. Pastor Adams also founded the First Assemblies of God that was a COGIC white church that later after Adams moved to Alabama joined the Assemblies. Elvis Presley's family attended first Assembly where he sang in the choir, and Elvis Presley liked to attend the COGIC Convocation to here is favor guitarist in the COGIC Utah Smith

In 1935, Bishop L.H. Ford, standing L-R second person was Mason's Public Relations Director who connected Political & Religious leaders National meetings

Bishop Louis Henry Ford was trained by Mason to connect this African American organization to Political leaders during Plessy vs. Ferguson despite racial discrimination in America white attended Mason's National meetings from 1935 until today

In the 1950 audio recording, Mason states how L. P. Adams assisted him in finding the actual property where Mason's first church was located in Memphis, Tennessee. He recalls that in 1897 the Lord told him to get up on a tree stump, and he began to preach in the open air this is when L.P. Adams met Mason for the first time and came up to him to help him find a location for Mason's future church. L. P. Adams was the white individual who was a minister and attorney by trade who collaborated with Mason to establish a white and black interracial fellowship of churches under Mason's leadership. [44]

This white and black fellowship took place in and around 1909 under banner of Mason's Church of God in Christ organization with Mason as its leader. Bishop Charles Harrison Mason, Leonard P. Adam (white), and William Holt (white) who established the Equal Right of Authority By-Law within the Pentecostal Church of God in Christ organization that contradicted the American jurisprudence of Plessy vs. Ferguson of 1896. [45]

Mason believed that God had called him to gather whites and blacks despite the American jurisprudence of Plessy vs. Ferguson of 1896, which made racial segregation legal in America. L. P. Adams's involvement with Mason showed up also when he testified on Mason's behalf when C.P. Jones tried to strip Mason of his local church in Memphis, Tennessee. [46]

During the court trial, the cross-examining attorney questioned L. P. Adams about his perspective on interracial worship he did not deny his belief, but stated that the gospel of Jesus Christ had no discrimination concerning race.

ENDNOTES

Chapter 4: Enlightenment and Betrayal

1.Burgess, Stanley M., and McGee, Gary B., *Dictionary of Pentecostal and Charismatic Movements*, Published by Zondervan, Grand Rapids, MI, 1988, Page 586.

3. James Courts, *The History and Life Work of Bishop C.H. Mason*, Privately Published: Memphis, TN, 191, Page 26.

4. Elijah Hill, *The Azusa Revival, Wrapped in Swaddling Clothes, Lying in a Manger Centennial Edition* 2006 Independently Published, Page 66.

5. Ibid. Page 66

6. William J. Seymour Editor, *The Apostolic Faith Newsletters Vol. 1-Vol II No. 13*, September 1906-1908, Republished by The Apostolic Faith Gospel Mission 1906-1909.

7. Elijah Hill, *The Azusa Revival, Wrapped in Swaddling Clothes, Lying in a Manger Centennial Edition.* 2006 Independently Published, Page 46.

8. Ibid., Page 49

9. David D. Daniels, "God Makes no Differences in Nationality: The Fashioning of a New Racial/Nonracial Identity at the Azusa Street Revival," in *Enrichment Journal*, ed Gary R. Allen and Rich Knoth, (Springfield, Missouri) Issue Spring 2006, Vol. 11, No. 1, Pg. 72-76.

10. James Courts, *The History and Life Work of Bishop C.H. Mason*, Privately Published: Memphis, TN, 1919, Page 26.

11. Ibid., Page 26.

12. Ibid., Page 27

13. Elijah Hill, "*The Azusa Revival, Wrapped in Swaddling Clothes, Lying in a Manger Centennial Edition.*" 2006 Independently Published, Page 69.

14. Ibid., Page 69

15. Ibid., Page 71

16. Minutes of the 12th Annual Holy Convocation, Church of God in Christ, Memphis, TN (November 1919), p. 13-14. Files of Geraldine Wright, Southfield, Michigan.

17. Elijah Hill, *The Azusa Revival, Wrapped in Swaddling Clothes, Lying in a Manger Centennial Edition.* 2006 Independently Published, Page 73.

18. James Courts, *The History and Life Work of Bishop C.H. Mason*, Privately Published: Memphis, TN, 191, Page 28.

19. Ibid., Page 28

20. Elijah Hill, *The Azusa Revival, Wrapped in Swaddling Clothes, Lying in a Manger Centennial Edition.* 2006 Independently Published, Page 74.

21. Ibid., Page 76

22. Ibid., Page 77

23. Ibid., Page 77

24. William J. Seymour Editor, *The Apostolic Faith Newsletters" Vol. 1-Vol II No. 13,* September 1906-1908, Republished by the Apostolic Faith Gospel Mission 1906-1909.

25. Bishop Ithiel C. Clemmons, *Bishop C.H. Mason and the roots of the Church of God in Christ,* Publisher: Pneuma Life Publishing, Bakersfield, California, 93389, and Page 29

26. Douglas J. Nelson, *For Such a Time as This: The Story of Bishop William J. Seymour and the Azusa Street Revival, a search for Pentecostal/Charismatic Roots,* (Ph.D. diss, University of Birmingham, England, May 1981), 196-199.

27. James Courts, *The History and Life Work of Bishop C.H. Mason,* Privately Published: Memphis, TN, 1919, Page 26.

28. Charles H. Pleas, *Fifty Years of Achievement: Church of God in Christ* Privately Published: Kansas City, KS, 1955, Page 6.

29. Ibid., Page 7

30. Deposition of C.H. Mason taken April 27, 1908, case #14770, Chancery Court of Shelby County, Tennessee, Frank Avant vs. C.H. Mason, pp. 99-101.

31. Ibid., Page 2

32. Bishop Ithiel C. Clemmons, *Bishop C.H. Mason and the roots of the Church of God in Christ,* Publisher: Pneuma Life Publishing, Bakersfield, California, 93389, Page 65.

33. Ibid., Page 65

34. Deposition of C.H. Mason taken April 27, 1908, case #14770, Chancery Court of Shelby County, Tennessee, Frank Avant vs. C.H. Mason, pp. 96.

35. Elijah Hill, *The Azusa Revival, Wrapped in Swaddling Clothes, lying in a Manger Centennial Edition.* 2006 Independently Published, Page 78.

36. Vinson Synan, *The Holiness-Pentecostal Movement in the U.S.,* Publisher: William B. Erdmans, Grand Rapids, MI, 1971.

37. C. F. Range Editor, *Church of God In Christ Official Manuel,* Publisher Church of God In Christ Publishing Board. 1973, Page XXIX.

38. Deposition of C.H. Mason taken April 27, 1908, case #14770, Chancery Court of Shelby County, Tennessee, Frank Avant vs. C.H. Mason, pp. 97-98.

39. Deposition of C.H. Mason taken April 27, 1908, case #14770, Chancery Court of Shelby County, Tennessee, Frank Avant vs. C.H. Mason, pp. 99-101.

40. Ibid., Page 2

41. Ibid., Page 3

42. Ibid., Page 3

43. Calvin S. Mc Bride, *Walking Into A New Spirituality*, Publisher iUniverse, Lincoln, Nebraska, 2007, Page 144-146.

44. Elijah L. Hill. (Copyright year) 2012. Title DVD Recording Follow Peace With All Men. Reproduction of Audio on DVD, Arlington, Texas. Original date of this audio recording was 1950 Bishop Charles Harrison Mason's personal sermon. Memphis, TN.

45. Paul S. Carter, *Heritage of Holiness (History of First Assembly of Memphis, Tennessee)*, Privately Published: Memphis, TN, 1991, Page 25.
46. Ibid., Page 25
47. Deposition of C.H. Mason taken April 27, 1908, case #14770, Chancery Court of Shelby County, Tennessee, Frank Avant vs. C.H. Mason, pp. 99-101.

Chapter 5—Teamwork Made the Dream Work

Bishop Mason retained the true essence of ministry, like an apostle of the first century church by nurturing and encouraging the releasing of men and women's spiritual gifts. He remained true to Christ by allowing an environment that perfected the saints for the work of the ministry. Bishop Mason's goal was to fully incorporate the five-fold ministry (Ephesians 4:11, 12) into his newly formed organization.

Today many individuals acknowledge the call to be an apostle in the Body of Christ. However, one key issue is that many carry the title, but do not understand the essence of the mantle of an apostle. The first century apostle groomed the disciples through the Word of God, not the doctrines of the Scribes and Pharisees. Committing to faithful men what the Lord Jesus had taught them. For the Lord Jesus rose up twelve successors (the one He lost was replaced) by spending time perfecting them for their future work of the ministry. He impressing upon them to stay focused on their relationship to their Father in Heaven by seeking first the Kingdom of God and His righteousness.

Unfortunately, the focus of many in the Body of Christ today is personal ambitions in the ministry, rather than perfecting laborers to win souls for God's Kingdom. The state of the Body of Christ is that we are too busy *serving* God (when in fact we are actually fulfilling our own selfish motives) instead of taking the time to *commune* with Him.[1] We have replaced true service with building a *name for ourselves*. Our true purpose is to bring souls into God's Kingdom. Tragically, the average Christian does not know how to lead a person to Christ; we have left this task for ministers and pastors during traditional sermons on Sundays. Some ministers do not even focus anymore on fulfilling the great commission, and are failing to be witnessing agents for the Lord of the Harvest.

However, Bishop C.H. Mason was one of the greatest examples of an apostle in the twentieth-century Pentecostal movement. He recognized the vital importance of prayer to keep the lifeblood of his ministry flowing. He greatly desired to maintain the essence of his Azusa Street experience, and to duplicate a prayerful church that society would *have* to recognize as a peculiar people for God's glory. The spiritual base of New Testament ministry that was birth out of prayer, fasting and waiting for the promise of the Father in the upper room. Acts 1:14 says, *"These all continued with one accord in prayer and supplication."* Mason essentially took a suppressed generation of slaves and sons of ex-slaves, who had upon them the spirit of division, and made them *one* through the power of prayer. Bishop Mason wanted to break the generational curse of division and tribal infighting that can be traced all the way back to Africa. It is recorded that he would pray, "Satan, I bind you and cast the devil out of their minds." Mason's goal was to pray fervently that they might be *one* with the Father in Heaven, and with one another.

There were many recorded times of how Bishop Charles Harrison Mason dealt with division and disagreement within his organization. One example is that when he learned of disputes amongst his national leaders, he would never give verbal feedback. He would just fall on his knees requesting that they pray, he would pray fervently for hours until the brothers got tired of praying, and as a result would confess, "God has fixed our hearts." We do not need to pray anymore Bishop Mason. The problem we had is resolved." Mother Lillian Brooks Coffey, who came up as a little girl under Mason's Saints Home church in Memphis, Tennessee, was very knowledgeable of this leadership style. She stated, "Many times I would observe him dealing with disagreements and infighting amongst the brethren by falling to his knees before addressing the dispute." He demonstrated to the brothers that some things must be taken to the Lord in prayer. Only the power of God could bring total peace to any situation. [3]

Elder WM. B. HOLT

One of the Overseers

OF THE CHURCH OF GOD IN CHRIST

Elder Wm. B. Holt was born in Fort Worth, Texas, April 15, 1880. Was converted in a Baptist School in Redlands, Cal. in 1901. At Camp Meeting in Downey, Cal., he received the grace of sanctification. In 1903 he joined the Nazarene Church, and was licensed to preach, and entered the Nazarene Bible College, as a divinity student. In 1914 he received the Baptism of the Holy Ghost, and in 1916 was appointed an Overseer in the Church of God in Christ by C. H. Mason, Chief Overseer.

5

In 1917, taken from the FBI files in Washington they removed it from the Church of God in Christ Manuel of 1917 a biography of Overseer William Henry Holt (white). Overseer William Holt was overseer of California under the African American Church of God in Christ organization.

Bishop Mason put into action the Biblical truth found in James 5: 16, *"Confess your faults one to another, and pray one for another, that ye may be healed. The effectual fervent prayer of a righteous man availeth much."* Many of them suppressed and mistreated within American society. They wanted to go their own independent way, but Bishop Mason was determined to make a divided people *one in Christ.* Another one of his famous Scriptures that he would quote is in I Chronicles 7:16, which states, *"If my people, which are called by my name, shall humble themselves, and pray, and seek my face, and turn from their wicked ways; then will I hear from heaven, and will forgive their sin, and will heal their land."* Bishop Mason believed totally that God's written Word was *the* effective guide to address the problems and ills of his people.

The power of prayer continued to bless his ministry on an even wider scale. During the Jim Crow period, not only did Bishop Mason bring together men of his own race, but contradicted America's racist views by allowing whites to receive his ordination and creating opportunities for interracial fellowship amongst *all* Pentecostals. He already had white followers like Elder James Delk, Leonard. P. Adams and William B. Holt who Mason appointed as his national recording secretary. William Holt held the national position within Mason's organization for over twenty-five years.[5]

In Gary Don McElhany's dissertation, "The South Aflame: A History of the Assemblies of God in the Gulf Region," he stated surrounding the earlier interaction of Assembly of God (AG) founders early involvement with Bishop Mason an African American minister before they began denying later their interracial fellowship with African Americans because of fear of violating Jim Crow laws. It reads:

"For instance, Mack M. Pinson reported that he and H.G. Rogers heard white evangelist G.B. Cashwell in Memphis in 1907. After Cashwell left town, they visited Mason's congregation where they witnessed a number of people receive the baptism in the Holy Spirit and speak in tongues. That night, Pinson and Rodgers prayed in their hotel room and spoke in tongues for the first time."[7]

According to Flowers, one of the earlier pioneers of the Assembly of God, he writes (re: Mason's ordination of H.A. Gross),

> "In the latter part of 1907, H. A. Gross had gone to Arkansas where he met Elder C. H. Mason, the General Overseer of the newly organized Church of God in Christ. Brother Gross accepted the courtesies of that organization and was issued credentials, which were recognized by the railroads. With the consent of Elder Mason, a white organization was formed, using the name "Church of God in Christ" and credentials were issued to E.N. Bell and a few other ministers."[8]

Also Grant Wacker's book, *Heaven Below: Early Pentecostals and American Culture*, (the interracial fellowship of the early AG founders, H.G. Rogers and Mack M. Pinson), states:

> "Pinson and Rodgers later became founding members of the Assemblies of God. It is significant that these white ministers from the Deep South were open to attending a black church in their search for spiritual truth."[9]

Regrettably, the AG went through an evolutionary change, and began to conform to the social mores of the racist views of American society that did not exist among the early Pentecostals at the Azusa Street Mission's Revival. In 1939, as recorded in the minutes of an Assemblies of God meeting (when they voted to agree not to ordain African Americans within their organization), it is stated:

"The body voted to express disapproval of the ordaining of colored men to the ministry and recommend that when those of the colored race apply for ministerial recognition, license to preach only be granted to them with instructions that they operate within the bounds of the District in which they are licensed; and if they desire ordination, refer them to the colored organizations."[10]

The AG began to move away from the multicultural worship and fellowship, which God had established at the Azusa Street Revival. A letter written by Flowers to Pinson reveals the real reason for racial separation amongst the white and black Pentecostals. Pinson states, "I know that Arkansas and other southern states have a Jim Crow law that stated that colored and whites can't work under the same charter. If that was done, the white Church of God in Christ was not legal, because they would have to have a charter of their own."[11]

Their dilemma was whether to maintain fellowship with the COGIC, or to assimilate and go along with Plessy vs. Ferguson, which upheld segregation as standard of the day for America's racial bias. Further contradictions reveal that when the Assembly of God separated themselves from the black Church of God in Christ in 1914, their founders invited Bishop Charles H. Mason to preach at their opening meeting. If there was no connection, as some present day white scholars proclaim, why invite an African American to bless your movement at its inception. This event is documented in the April 20, 1914, edition of the *Word and Witness* publication stating, *"Hot Springs Assembly; God's Glory Present."* One of the white participants at the Hot Springs meeting recalled that Mason "brought a glorious message" and that "there were a number of colored folks present at this meeting."[12] The Church of God in Christ historian, Bishop Ithiel Clemmons, described this event in more detail, since he had several interviews with our founder surrounding certain instances not fully described by white Pentecostals. He stated, "In 1914, the Assemblies of God organized as a white denomination, separated from the Church of God in Christ. In the second week in April of that year, Mason traveled to Hot Springs, Arkansas along with L. P. Adams and William Holt, to attend the first annual meeting of the Assemblies of God. He sang his spontaneous, improvisation of spiritual songs that Daniel Payne wrote in 1879 called "corn-field ditties." L. P. Adams and William Holt were two of the white ministers that supported Bishop Mason maintaining a white and black fellowship despite the Assembly of God's decision to separate from Mason's ministerial fellowship. In the Heritage Holiness history of the First Assembly of Memphis written by Paul S. Carter, page 25. He recorded how Mack Pinson was upset with L.P. Adams for drawing up the statement of faith paperwork within Mason's group and disseminating it to the Whites and Blacks because he felt he was going against the Jim Crow laws of the South. In Paul Carter's version of L. P. Adam's history he stated Adam's was supposed to be one of the speakers at the first council of the Assemblies along with Mason, but Pinson brought up an accusation surrounding L.P. Adams to cause the elders to reject him as speaker. Along with Mason's entourage also was the Saints Industrial, singers from Lexington, Mississippi. Mason bid the white leaders a warm farewell and gave them leave to void their Church of God in Christ credentials in order to switch to those of their new denomination, but Bishop Mason, L.P. Adams (white) and William Holt (white) continued on with the White and Black fellowship of Pentecostal under the Church of God in Christ organization."[13]

In spite of this separation, Bishop Charles Harrison Mason continued to believe in the Constitution of the United States that, "all men are created equal, endowed by their creator with certain unalienable rights." That with these is "life, liberty and pursuit of happiness," and for this reason he continued to embrace his white brothers and welcomed their fellowship with open arms. [14]

A LIST of the GENERAL OFFICIAL HEADS

of the

Church of God in Christ

ELDER C. H. MASON, Chief Overseer

871 Mississippi Ave., Memphis, Tenn.

STATE GENERAL OVERSEERS:

JUSTUS BOWE, 513 W. 24th St., Argenta, Ark.

E. M. PAGE, 3028 Thomas Ave., Dallas, Texas.

JEFF A. LEWIS, Natchez, Miss.

R. E. HART, 447 S. Church St., Jackson, Tenn.

D. BOSTICK, 2948 Market Street, St. Louis, Mo.

MACK E. JONES, Cleveland, Ohio.

HENRY FELTUS, 110 Lucy St., Baton Rouge, La.

S. T. SAMUEL, 3014 Roanoke ave. Newport News, Va.

E. R. DRIVER, 1527 E. 22nd street, Los Angeles, Cal.

D. J. YOUNG, 1918 N. Sixth st., Kansas City, Kan.

B. J. REECE, 237 S. Murry st., Atlanta, Ga.

J. S. RILEY, 198 E. 100th st., New York City, N. Y.

L. P. ADAMS, Box 58, Memphis, Tenn.

WM. B. HOLT, 309 Columbia Trust Building,

Los Angeles, Cal.

In 1917, taken from FBI files Washington they took it from the 1917 Church of God in Christ Manuel listed L.P. Adams and William Holt (white).

Bishop C.H. Mason continued in developing the prophetic purpose of the original Pentecostal Movement at Azusa Street Mission that was about the Democratization of all cultures no matter what their race or creed. Bishop Mason collaborated with one of his white followers creating what they called, "Philosophy *of God: the Brotherhood of Man Through the Holy Scriptures.*" What this information was about was Mason and Delk implementing strategies to challenge Plessy vs. Ferguson's segregation by Mason having James Delk a white brother within Mason's African American movement to present speeches to white groups to become open minded about having Bishop Mason presented at their white organizations. It stated within the booklet that true holiness, regardless of creed, color or race, meant that you could not discriminate against your Christian brothers and sisters, and maintain your true testimony that you were born again. Elder Delk's assignment as a white brother within the Church of God in Christ was to go out and preach to other white brothers and sisters. He was Bishop Mason's white representative within his African American denomination who proclaimed that Jim Crow laws were neither Christian nor Godly.[15] He believed that the entire Christian family, regardless of color, was God's family and to mistreat, hurt or put them down was in violation of Heaven's laws which superseded the earthly Jim Crow laws.

Around 1909, Bishop Mason appointed two whites as state overseers. L.P. Adams assigned to Memphis, Tennessee, and William B. Holt assigned to Los Angeles, California. These actions by Mason just further demonstrated interracial dynamics within Mason's ministry; which were in complete opposition to America's social standards and laws of Plessy vs. Ferguson separate but equal segregation laws in America's jurisprudences created in 1896.[16]

PHILOSOPHY AND DEMOCRACY

Philosophy of God as been preached through
Senior Bishop C. H. Mason for the
Past 62 years.

Philosophy and Democracy taught by the late
Franklin D. Roosevelt and his wife,
Mrs. Eleanor Roosevelt

December 7, 1945

Written by Dr. James L. Delk,
Hopkinsville, Kentucky

Provided from the Archives of Bishop A.D. Baxter, Sr.

In 1945, Pastor James Delk wrote this book to platform Bishop Charles Harrison Mason's Philosophy of God surrounding black & white integration through the gospel. James Delk used this book to present to white audiences to platform discussions surrounding Plessy vs. Ferguson or Jim Crow was not biblical. Pastor James Delk was sharing with white audiences that Bishop C.H. Mason had been preaching this democratization of Christianity for over sixty-two years before Plessy vs. Ferguson in 1896.

Bishop Charles Harrison Mason set the standard for civil liberties within America by holding fast to the first Amendment to the Constitution of the United States, which was freedom of Assembly in religion. By Mason assembling with white Americans, and allowing them to be a part of his African American denomination from 1908-1955 right before the wake of Dr. Martin Luther King Jr.,'s Civil Rights Movement. When Brown vs. The Board of Education resulted in the Supreme Court rescinding the old segregation laws that Mason was in conflict with up until 1955 under the banner of his Church of God in Christ national ministry. Mason lived to see his dream happen six years before he died in 1961 for over fifty years he had boldly been in opposition to segregation through his Church of God in Christ Pentecostal Movement prior to the Civil Rights Movement in America.

Another situation where a white man demonstrated public support to an African American Bishop Mason was L.P. Adams who supported Mason during C.P. Jones' conspiracy. In his deposition, the prosecutor questioned Adams along the line, "If his church was interracial. His response was, "We don't restrict ourselves to the baptism, but the love of God and a pure heart." [17] This was not the first time L.P. Adams supported his Pentecostal African American friends publically as a Pentecostal in legal situations. He also accompanied G.B. Cashwell, Mack M. Pinson and Glen Cook down to the Memphis Police Station to get one of Bishop Mason's African American members out of jail for speaking in tongues while on the job.[18]

All four of these white pioneers of the Modern Day Pentecostal Movement assisted in conducting and participated in services at Bishop Charles H. Mason's African American church in Memphis, Tennessee. Mack M. Pinson, seven years later, became one of the founding fathers of the Assembly of God organization. He followed G. B. Cashwell to Memphis, Tennessee, to assist Glen Cook in conducting a meeting at Bishop Charles Harrison Mason's church prior to Mason's return from Azusa. Both Glen Cook and G. B. Cashwell knew each other because they both received their doctrinal teaching and baptism of the Holy Spirit experience at Azusa Street under an African American in 1906 who was Pastor William J. Seymour. [19]

The AG has the notes of J. Roswell Flowers in 1950 who documented information surrounding Howard Gross in relation to whites and blacks working together. He stated from Gross's unpublished dairies stated:

> "In the latter part of 1907, H. A. Gross had gone to Arkansas where he met Elder C.H. Mason, the General Overseer of the newly organized Church of God in Christ. Brother Gross accepted the courtesies of that organization and was issued credentials, which were recognized by the southern railroads. With the consent of Elder Mason, a white organization was formed, using the name *Church of God in Christ* and credentials were issued to E. N. Bell and a few other ministers."[20]

Flowers also wrote a letter to Mack M. Pinson affirming his account of the whites' receiving credentials from Mason, it states:

> "H.A. Gross did keep a diary and I have gleaned quite a number of facts from him. He received the baptism under Chas F. Parham in 1903. In the latter part of 1907, he visited Elder Mason of the Churches of God in Christ and received credentials from the Negro body. He obtained from Elder Mason permission to issue papers using that name *Churches of God in Christ* for the white work in Texas."[21]

In 1910, Professor James Courts the first to start a school for the education of youth in the Church of God in Christ, which later on Dr. Arenia Mallory took over

In 1965, this ceremony was held about Saints Industrial finally receiving their College accreditation in Lexington, MS L-R, Annie Ford, Bishop L.H. Ford, Governor Mississippi, Dr. Mallory, Presiding Bishop J. O. Patterson, unknown

In 1960's Saints Junior College how the campus looked then

In 1935, Saints Industrial School Singers They traveled with Dr. Mallory and Mary McLeod Bethune to the White House on many occasions.

Classes held at Saints Industrial

G. B. Cashwell, the Apostle of the South, talks about his change of conscience surrounding interracial worship while at the Azusa Street Mission where he went to receive the Baptist of the Holy Spirit. Initially, he did not want blacks to lay hands on him; but after God's conviction, he allowed them and afterward then received the Baptism of the Holy Ghost. Now we find him, Pinson a (AG founder) assisting Cook and Adams with the release of one of Mason's members from jail resulting from a revival the white brothers are conducting at Bishop Mason's African American church.

The *Memphis Commercial Appeal Newspaper* ran a front-page article titled "Negro Houseboy Makes Funny Talk at Police Station." The secular newspaper documented that white men Glen Cook, G.B Cashwell, L.P. Adams and Mack M. Pinson had come down to get the Negro boy released. They explained to the chief of Police at the police station that he had received the Holy Ghost while they were conducting their meeting at Bishop Mason's church in Memphis, Tennessee.[22]

All of these facts, being indisputable, validate Bishop Mason having a relationship and fellowshipping with whites in worship and within the organization of the COGIC.[23] In 1919, Professor Courts the first individual to write a biography on Bishop Charles Harrison Mason documented that there were seventeen state overseers fifty black and two white within Bishop Mason's organization at that time:

D.J. Young, 1958 N. Sixth St., Kansas City, Kansas
R.E. Hart, 447 S. Church St., Jackson, Tennessee
J. Bowe, Geridge, Arkansas
Elder S. Rice, Lexington, Mississippi
D. Bostic, 2948, Market St., St. Louis, Missouri
B.I. Ieece, 237 S. Murry St., Atlanta, Georgia
E.R. Driver, 1527 E. 22nd St., *Los* Angeles, California
Henry Felters, 110 Lucy St., Baton Rouge, Louisiana
E.M. Page, 3028 Thomas Ave., Dallas, Texas
I.S. Riley, 198 E. 100th St., New York City
Mack Jones, 1801 Colonial Court, Cleveland, Ohio

L.P. Adams, Memphis, Tennessee. (White State Overseer)
William B. Holt, 309 Columbia Bldg., Los Angeles, California
(White State Overseer)
S.T. Samuel, 3014 Roanoke Ave, Newport News, Virginia
V.M. Barker, 1727 Highland Ave., Kansas City, Missouri
G.W. Montear, 820 Lexington St., Norfolk, Virginia[24]

In 1919 in Professor Court's, book the first biography on Bishop Charles Harrison Mason it, list two white brothers as Overseers under Mason's African American organization L. P. Adams overseer of Memphis, TN and William Holt overseer of Lost Angeles, California all the other leaders listed have been identified as African Americans. However, Elder James Delk who became Bishop Mason's official spokesperson to the general white American population in the late 1930's. One of the books Delk wrote to facilitate Mason's social impact upon America, was *What the Southern White Minister Has to Say About the Colored Minister*, describes Bishop Mason's philosophy concerning true holiness that has no regard to creed, color, or race. The white minister James Delk worked along with Bishop C.H. Mason for over thirty years until his death spearheading Mason's "Philosophy of God campaign in America. He shared with white religious groups about the fact that the racial divide of Plessy vs. Ferguson or Jim Crowism was not biblically right, and these laws in America that fostered segregation were wrong according to the laws of Heaven. Pastor James Delk as a white Church of God in Christ pastor even ran for Governor of Tennessee his campaign slogan was, "You white people need to treat African American people right instead of discriminating against them." Pastor Delk and Bishop Mason as white and black Pentecostal leaders worked side by side collaborating with strategies to break down the walls of segregation in the South decades before the Civil Rights as a public protest Movement had even begun in America. This was one of Pastor Delk's speeches before many white congregations:[25]

"But bear in mind that either Brother Mason or myself believe in *segregation or Jim Crow*, but all people, either white or colored, do not see this in the same light that Brother Mason and myself see it.

This has all been accomplished because of the leadership in the person of Bishop C.H. Mason. I doubt if there has ever been a Minister who has lived since the day of the Apostles, who has shown the sweet spirit to all people, regardless of race, creed or color, or has preached with greater power than Brother Mason. We read of John and Charles Wesley, founders of Methodism, who were great men; we read of George Fox, founder of Quakerism, who was a great man; Reverend Campbell, founder of the Christian Church; and Roger Williams, founder of the Baptist Church who also were great men. I have met and heard Williams Booth, the founder of the Salvation Army; Brother Brazil, founder of the Nazarene Church; Brother Bell, founder of the Assembly of God; and Rev. Thomson of the Church of God. I have heard D.L. Moody preach and was personally acquainted with Aimee Semple McPherson for thirty years, Rev. Paul Reader and the late Billy Sunday."[26]

Elder Delk toured the United States as an Evangelist who was white, and he stayed with COGIC African American pastors in their homes, preached in COGIC churches and ate at their dinner tables. It was as if the Blood of the Lamb, as in the Azusa Street Revivals, had washed the color line away. Here is an account James Delk shared about his experiencing evangelism and fellowship with his African American brothers and sisters in the COGIC. Rev. James Delk a Church of God in Christ leader who was a white man live amongst African American and White American society to champion abolishing racial segregation.

The Triumph of the Black Church

Strategic Personnel helped Mason's Social/Political Platform in America
during Plessy vs. Ferguson to fight Racism/Sexist/Social Injustices

L.P. Adams co-created White   William Holt National Sec. Mason
Black Fellow with Mason   part White/Black Fellowship

Mother Lizzie Robinson Global-   Bishop L.H. Ford developed
ized COGIC Women Leadership   political relationship

James Delk, Spokesperson for   Dr. Arenia Mallory COGIC & Women's Club
Mason against Jim Crow 1939-65 Spokesperson for Mary McLeod Bethune

Elder Delk at the end of this presentation gives the reason for his proposed campaign against racism in America it was because he and Bishop Mason was against segregation and Jim Crow in America they took a bold position against the jurisprudence of America the Plessy vs. Ferguson legislation of 1896. Most scholars even African American focus on Mason's spirituality, but do not give him credit for his social and political approach to the right of African Americans under religious liberties and the right to assemble together despite their race according to the Constitution of the United States:

"I left home the 7th of June, 1944, and went to Cincinnati, Ohio, where I visited Mother and Brother Wiley's home, 906 West 7th St, and preached for Elder P.J. Bryant in his tent. I found Elder Bryant and his wife blessed people, and was treated royally by Elder Bryant and his wife and also Mother and Brother Wiley. I went from Cincinnati to Springfield, Ohio, and preached a couple of nights for Elder J.G. Jackson, pastor of the Church of God in Christ, and was entertained in Elder Jackson's home and found Elder Jackson, his wife and little Junior blessed people. I met Rev. Davis of the Church of God in Christ who immediately informed me of the State Convocation being held at Rev. Clemmon's church in Brooklyn, and he said that Senior Bishop Mason was there. I went immediately to Rev. Clemmon's Church, and as I arrived at the church door, there stood Rev. O.M. Kelly and Rev. Clemmons. We were glad to meet each other, and they were loyal to me in the convocation and had me preach on August 3rd which was my 41st anniversary in the Gospel. Bishop Mason was at that very same convocation and preached a powerful sermon, which he always does and all enjoyed him very much."[27]

"I hope that the reader, especially of the Colored race, will realize the significance of a white man writing about a colored man. The reader might say it makes no difference, but I say it does. For instance, if Joe Louis, the heavyweight champion were to write a book of praise about the white man it would prove of great significance and help among the colored people more than among the white people. No doubt, this book will prove of more significance among the white people than it will among the colored people. But bear in mind that neither Brother Mason nor myself believe in segregation or the Jim Crow system, but all people, either white or colored, do not see this in the same light that Brother Mason and myself see it."[28]

Delk also cites how he was able to get Bishop Mason some forty-one years later to run a camp meeting revival for him. This is his record of the event:

"Bishop Mason is still living and turning on his 80th year. To me he does not look any older than he did the first day I met him which was more than 41 years ago. He is as active as a man of 30 and the greatest leader in prayer I have ever met. In 1931, I was the head of a religious colony four miles east of Sullivan, Missouri, 58 miles southwest of St. Louis, on U.S. Highway 66. I secured Brother Mason to come to my place and conduct a ten-day Camp Meeting. People came to these meetings from every walk of life by the thousands."[29]

The Church of God in Christ has chosen for their Spiritual leader the simple title of Overseer, taken from the Scriptural admonition to "feed the flock of God over whom the Holy Ghost hath made you Overseers." Acts 20:28. While they are not Bishops in name they are in fact. Being vested with all the ecclesiastical power of a Bishop. Namely, to ordain Elders, commission evangelists, organize and dedicate churches and to preside at the Annual State Convocation of the church.

THE GENERAL OVERSEER

The General Overseer corresponds in power and authority to a Presiding Bishop, having general supervision of the church and presiding at the official meetings of the Overseers.

EQUAL IN POWER AND AUTHORITY

Many denominations have made a distinction between their colored and white members. Some have advised electing colored officials to preside over colored assemblies, while others have refused to elevate any colored elder to the episcopacy or any office corresponding to it having equal power with the white bishops. This has led to many misunderstandings and has caused the organizing of many separate colored denominations.

The Church of God in Christ recognizes the fact that all believers are one in Christ Jesus and all its members have equal rights. Its Overseers, both colored and white, have equal **power and authority** the church.

In 1917, FBI Files taken from Church of God in Christ Manuel part called Equal in Power and Authority Bishop Mason his organization makes no distinction between races within his African American organization.

Charles Harrison Mason obviously left an indelible imprint upon America's segregated society. His influential prayer and healing ministry had spread throughout the South, and it was typical of him to assemble with all white audiences to worship and conduct the services for them. During this time, the lynching of other black ministers was common if attempting to cross-racial segregation barriers matter of fact most minister would not because their very life was threatened.

Not only was Bishop Mason influential in establishing interracial worship opportunities, but he was also one of the pioneers of women in ministerial roles. The women of the church played a vital role in founding congregations, and in the absence of a pastor would function in the teaching role and have acting charge of these newly starting congregations. He realized he needed a woman capable of organizing his national women's work. He heard of Lizzie Wood and her and Mason meets at Dermott Baptist College. [30] He shared with her about his vision and baptism of the Holy Spirit at the Azusa Street Revival and how the Baptist faith did not believe that the God-given promise of Acts 1: 4, 5 was for the present-day Christians. Lizzie's hunger for God caused her to accept these Scriptural truths and the testimony of Bishop Mason. He laid hands on her and she received the Holy Ghost. The Baptist Academy did not accept the doctrinal belief of the Baptism of the Holy Ghost; therefore, they excommunicated Ms. Woods from the Academy. They excommunicated her since she began to believe in the doctrine of Pentecost. [31] In November of 1911, while she attended the fourth Annual National Holy Convocation; General Overseer C. H. Mason as the first National General Overseer of Women's Work appointed her. Unlike most of his male contemporaries, Bishop Mason believed that women should be out front in leadership roles cooperating alongside men in church work.

Mason's vision was that women leaders would work alongside male leaders, governing, organizing and facilitating other female's leadership roles. There are two primary factors that influenced his belief: (1) the historic fact that in African culture, the senior women in the family were looked to for a strong leadership role, (2) Mason witnessed at the Azusa Street Revival the gender issue being washed away during the outpouring of the Holy Spirit.[32] Within his organization the women functioned in leadership and preaching roles alongside their male counterparts assisting them in the work of God's Kingdom. The men may have wanted to see the women only as teachers and not preachers, but Bishop Mason assisted in the vanishing of these historical and cultural differences.

Even though Mason skillfully allowed this coexistence of men and women in ministry, he also maintained God's divine order of male headship, as a "checks and balance system." Women in ministry respected their male overseers, along with their female supervisors. Mother Lizzie Robinson's ministry worked under the support mechanism of a Pentecostal denominational structure. This was the first time in history that this pivotal and unique occurrence appeared in religious history. These women essentially became God's leading ladies; they were spiritual *Deborah's* that paved the way for establishing women's visibility within traditional denominational structures in the Pentecostal and broader Protestant communities.

This moment in history parallels the Scripture in Judges 4:8, which says, "*And Barak said unto her, if thou wilt go with me, then I will go: but if thou wilt not go with me, then I will not go. And she said, I will surely go with thee, notwithstanding the journey that thou takest shall not be for thine honour; for the Lord shall sell Sisera into the hand of a woman.*" Bishop Mason's prayer was to have *Deborahs* at his side who were able to teach, direct and organize another army of Azusa Street Praying Sisters who would be willing to join him in spiritual battle and willing to go to war on the battlefield for his Lord and Savior Jesus Christ. Mason realized what his contemporaries did not, the benefit of creating opportunities for women to work alongside men.[33]

The Triumph of the Black Church

In 1932, seated L-R, Mother   In 1910, Mother Lizzie
Lizzie Robinson and Bishop   Robinson & only daughter
Charles Harrison Mason   Ida F. Baker

In 1960, Women's Convention   In 1946, Mary McLeod Bethune

In 1965, African Missionary Beatrice Lott builds school

Mason while at the Azusa Revival experienced the ministry of sisters like Lucy F. Farrow, who was the niece of the famous abolitionist-journalist, Fredrick Douglas. The Pentecostal scholars acknowledge Lucy's ministry in the history of the Azusa Street Revival as a great woman of prayer. Who had the New Testament Apostle Peter's gift of the laying on of hands when individuals would receive the Holy Ghost.[34] There are testimonies of hundreds of important future leaders of the Pentecostal Movement, who instantly received the Baptism of the Holy Ghost as Miss Farrow laid hands on them. Many of these individuals were men that were hungry and sought for the first century church "Day of Pentecost" experience.

At that time, it was acceptable for the women to act as spiritual midwives assisting in birthing forth God's divine oracles into the earth. Many of these same male leaders later took a different position towards women in ministry allowing the sexism of America to suppress the effect of women in ministry. God did not ask the permission of the men when He orchestrated what took place at the Azusa Street Mission. Mason refused to go the same direction as others and welcomed the sisters walking alongside the brothers in building God's Kingdom. During the Azusa Street Revival, did not God place white and black women strategically in position to take the lead in distributing the message of Pentecost throughout this country? This is the Lord's doing; and it should be marvelous in our eyes!

Mason realized that if you wanted to promote something, tell it to a woman and she will spread the news all around. He also understood what Jesus did after his resurrection when He first met Mary Magdalene at the tomb. In John 20:17,18, it says, *"But go to my brethren, and say unto them...Mary Magdalene came and told the disciples that she had seen the Lord, and that he had spoken these things unto her."* The first publishing of the gospel started with a woman. God entrusted the initial message (He is Risen!) to a loving and faithful woman who would have done anything for her Lord.

pastor and they will not be permitted to teach if it is found out that she talks with the weaker ones of the church who fight the pastorship.

9 No sister who has two or three husbands unlawfully according to the doctrines of the church of God in Christ can be a Missionary.

10 Workers requesting some sister to work, send your request to your pastor or State Mother.

11 All sisters applying for License to do Missionary Work must come before the State Mother's Board with recommendations from their pastor.

12 These rules are to be read in Bible Board Meetings.

All members and all Missionaries in good and regular standing with the Church of God in Christ must work in unity with the State Overseer, State Mother and Pastor.

ELDER C. H. MASON, Senior Bishop
MOTHER LIZZIE ROBINSON
General Supervisor of Women's Work

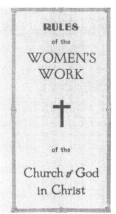

RULES

of the

WOMEN'S WORK

✝

of the

Church of God in Christ

In 1993 Street Mother Robinson   In 1926 Women's Work Rules

Stretch of Erskine Now Lizzie Robinson Avenue

In 1993 Lizzie Robinson Installed   In 1945 last letter Mother Robinson

Mrs. Robinson and her husband, Edward, started the first Nebraska congregation in Omaha in 1916. Both are deceased.

That was 10 years after she helped Bishop Charles Harrison Mason found the church in Lexington, Miss. Erskine Street from 24th to 27th Streets will be renamed in honor of Mrs. Robinson. Among the supporters of the change were Pastor Elijah L. Hill, state historian for the church.

The predominantly black Church of God in Christ has 3.7 million members worldwide and is the second largest black church in the United States. The church has 16 congregations in Nebraska, including 13 in Omaha.

Robinson Memorial Church, 2318 N. 26th St., is named after the Robinsons. In June, the council designated the church and the former Robinson residence at 2864 Corby St. as historic landmarks. The designations were approved in February by the Landmarks Heritage Preservation Commission.

Omaha World-Herald
Wednesday, August 5, 1992   15

Council Says: Here's to You, Mrs. Robinson

BY JOE BRENNAN
WORLD-HERALD STAFF WRITER

Omaha's newest street name is Lizzie Robinson Avenue.

The City Council voted Tuesday to rename a three-block stretch of Erskine Street for the woman who helped organize the Church of God in Christ.

■ Tax increases and job cuts draw fire at Omaha budget hearing. Page 23.
■ Lottery and sales-tax money will help LaVista double its budget. Page 17.

Nebraska. The council approved the ordinance unanimously.

"Lizzie Robinson is significant historically for her role as organizer of the women's ministry for the church," said City Planning Director Gary Pryor.

1992 Elder Hill obtains St Name   In 1945 last photo Robinson

Moreover, in spite of cultural biases, Bishop Mason lifted the glass ceiling by allowing extraordinary leadership development opportunities for women of his organization.[35]

Mother Lizzie Robinson built an elaborate women's ministry for the Church of God in Christ from 1911-1945 when she died, while at the Memphis Holy Convocation the year that Mason Temple was completed. To her memorial I had obtained a street named after her in Omaha, Nebraska in 1992 called Lizzie Robinson Ave, her home called the Lizzie Robinson House has been placed on the Federal Registry of historical places noting that her history was a vital part of America's religious history. Bishop C.H. Mason had a very keen ability to identify team members that would have a long-term impact upon the organization and the world around them. One of the essential personnel was Dr. Arenia C. Mallory who he appointed over Saint's Industrial School in Lexington, Mississippi his organizations educational division.[36] She becomes a very significant player in the social activism involvement of the Church of God in Christ in the Women's Club Movement in the early 20th Century.

Mallory forms an alliance with one of the most notable women in Pre-Civil Rights in America Mary McLeod Bethune who was the founder and president of the National Council of Negro Women. Mary McLeod Bethune wanted an alliance with the Church of God in Christ Women Department because their organization was the only Protestant African American religious organization that allowed women in leadership roles. During the 1930's they created a nationally network of female leadership throughout the United States to assist Mary Bethune in jump-starting her new organization the National Council of Negro Women. Dr. Mallory becomes one of the founding members of Bethune's women club movement, and Bethune identified with her because she and Mallory were the only two African American women that were presidents of colleges in the United States.[37]

In 1946, at Church of God in Christ World Headquarters standing L-R, Mary McLeod Bethune, and Mother Lillian Brooks-Coffey at her installation service, and Mary Bethune understood that the Church of God in Christ was the only African American religious organization that had allowed women to organize independently with their denomination and she needed the partnership for her National Council of Negro Women's organization.

Mallory's partnership with Bethune gave the Church of God in Christ organization total access to the white house by way of Mallory being Bishop C.H.
Mason's female representative on education. Bethune was a friend to President Franklin D. Roosevelt's wife Eleanor Roosevelt the first lady of the United States. Mary Bethune was the only black woman who was a part of Roosevelt's "New Deal" "Black Cabinet" that began to accept blacks in presidential cabinet positions in mid-1930. In August 7, 1936, Bethune once in the White House collaborated with Robert Weaver the first African American that President Roosevelt placed over the U.S. Housing Authority. Together they organized the Federal Governments' Council of Negro Affairs, which became responsible for recruiting the first 100 talented blacks place into presidential cabinet positions during Franklin Roosevelt's administration. [38]

Bethune in 1936 accepted the first paid cabinet position by an African America woman after having formed the National Council of Negro women in 1935 with Dr. Mallory of the Church of God in Christ at her side. Dr. Mallory, with her connections with the women of the Church of God in Christ under girded Bethune's movement with Mother Lillian Brooks-Coffey's assistance having a national network of women to draw from. Mallory became the international spokesperson for Mary McLeod Bethune as she became busy working with Washington, D.C., Mallory from the Church of God in Christ would speak on her behalf representing her at the International Women's Convention in Helsinki, Finland, and representing her at the United Nations in the 1940's. [39]

Bishop Charles Harrison Mason understood the dynamic of this partnership in the Church of God in Christ this is how they became visible within the broader society's social movement. His organization cultural dynamic was such that within the Church of God in Christ no leader would make a move without Bishop Mason's approval and blessings. The national leaders within the Church of God in Christ movement would always seek for Bishop

In 1951, L-R, Bishop C.H. Mason, Mother Lillian Brooks-Coffey, Mary
McLeod Bethune, Dr. Arenia Mallory at COGIC Women's Convention
Mary Bethune's partnership with the Church of God in Christ women along
With Dr. Arenia Mallory being co-founder of the National Council of Negro
Women and Bethune's personal Spokesperson Internationally.

In 1930's Mary McLeod Bethune visiting with Eleanor Roosevelt, and
Bethune entering the White House having more access than any other
African American.

Mason counsel before making these kinds of national decisions. As an African American twentieth Century denominational leader, he was strategic in his approach. Mason realized that women were a less threatening force to the larger white society, so he allowed his two main leaders Coffey and Mallory to involve his women's movement in social and political activities using their civic night services as their platform.

The Pre-Civil Rights movement had already begun within the United States Government with the Roosevelt administration integrating the first 100 talented African Americans in Presidential cabinet positions. Mary McLeod Bethune being the driving forces behind this first wave of integration in the White House cabinet positions for African Americans. Later in September 6, 1940, Bethune headed President Roosevelt's National Youth Administration's office, and ironically, Bethune was the only one of the black cabinet entrusted by the President to disbursement federal funds. Under Bethune's administration over a six-year period, she disbursed to African American youth for job training and college tuition over $600,000 in federal funding during the Great Depression. [40]

Many times when Bethune would attend meetings at the White House her friend Dr. Mallory of the Church of God in Christ accompanied her, and brought along the famous singing children from the Church of God in Christ Lexington Mississippi School to entertain the leaders at the White House. She often came along with Bethune for fundraisers for their respective colleges Bethune-Cookman and Saints Industrial School that Mallory was president over in Lexington, Mississippi. Bethune and Mallory teamed up many times traveling together to raise funds to maintain these respective schools. [41]

In 1930's President Roosevelt under pressure from A Phillip Randolph in 1930 has threatened to March On Washington Roosevelt integrated the Military

In 1960's A Phillip Randolph acknowledged for organizing the Dr. Martin Luther King's March on Washington by President J.F. Kennedy& L.B. Johnson.

In 1965, A. Phillip Randolph   In 1959, A. Phillip Randolph & Elenora

114

Another important figure in the Pre-Civil Rights in America was A. Phillip Randolph who called for the first "March on Washington" in 1941 to protest discrimination in the war industry. It was this outright protest that Bethune endorsed that caused the President of the United States Franklin Roosevelt to stop the march by implementing Executive Order 8802 the Fair Employment Act for the United States Military. The evolution of the Civil Rights movement had begun that would later become full blown in the "1960." It was actually A. Phillip Randolph who introduced the "March on Washington" concept to Dr. Martin Luther King, Jr., and it was his group and associates the structured the march as they had already done in the early 1940s.[42]

Bishop Charles Harrison Mason initiated civil rights or civil liberties in 1917, when he telegraphed President Woodrow Wilson to discuss his African American religious organization's conscientious objection to the Selective Service Act of 1917. The founder of the Church of God in Christ was permitted by the War Department to be exempt after Mason's visit to Washington, D.C. to visit the President who could not make the meeting because he had to leave meet World leaders to develop the, "Trendy of Versailles" in Paris. Therefore, the war department official worked out the details with Mason on the religious civil liberties of his religious organization based upon the First Amendment to the Constitution of America under freedom of religion.[43]

Mason's court case was at the forefront of spearheading religious civil liberties in America his pacifist case was one of the first tried by the United States Attorney General's office in the United States in 1918. Mason's case was one of the first court cases surrounding many pacifism in other religions that would go to jail for over 10 years and over twenty were sentenced to death for treason for violating of the Espionage Act of 1918.

In 1950's Mary McLeod Bethune was the first African American to get
Monuments build in the Washington Park area for her Humanitarian work

In 1950's Mary McLeod Bethune was the only one of President Roosevelt's
African American Black Cabinet leaders to give out federal funding under
her National Youth Program.

The Civil Liberties Union today as we know it started in 1920's because of World War I and President Woodrow Wilson misuse of the Espionage Act and the Seditious Act that violated many religious American's civil and religious liberties in America. Bishop Charles Harrison Mason's court case was one of the early court cases that the Federal Government did not win because of the spiritual power in his life was so connected that God had protected him from death. The Civil Liberties Union was established represent people whose civil liberties were violated by the American government.

The Pre-Civil Rights movement had already begun through civil liberties through Bishop Charles H. Mason. He supported freedom of religion during World War I and freedom to Assembly having whites of blacks in his religious movement opposing Plessy vs. Ferguson of 1896 that authorized the segregation of whites and blacks in American law. Mary McLeod Bethune started Pre-Civil Rights inside the White House by pushing for "The Black Cabinet" during the "30's" during President Roosevelt's administration. It was A. Phillip Randolph who started the social civil rights movement within the black community to implement the equal pay for blacks in the railroad business, and who implemented the "March on Washington" concept in the "40's."

America's first phase of the Civil Rights movement started from 1896-1954 with Plessy vs. Ferguson in 1896, and the second phase started when Brown vs. Board of Education repealed Plessy vs. Ferguson in 1955. Then the Modern Day Civil Rights movement began from 1955-1968 after the assassination of Dr. Martin Luther King, Jr.,

ENDNOTES

Chapter 5: Teamwork Makes the Dream Work

1. Elijah L. Hill, *Women Come Alive*, Arlington, Texas, P.O. Box 181937, (Independently Published), May, 2005, Page 56, 57.
2. William J. Seymour Editor, *The Apostolic Faith Newsletters* Published by the Azusa Street Mission. Vol. 1 No. 6, February-March 1907, Page 30.
3. Minutes of the 12th Annual Holy Convocation, Church of God in Christ, Memphis, TN (November 1919), p. 13-14.
4. Burgess, Stanley M., and McGee, Gary B., *Dictionary of Pentecostal and Charismatic Movements*, Published by Zondervans, Grand Rapids, MI, 1988, Page 587.
5. James Courts, *The History and Life Work of Bishop C.H. Mason*, Privately Published: Memphis, TN, 1919, Page 32.
6. Burgess, Stanley M., and McGee, Gary B., *Dictionary of Pentecostal and Charismatic Movements*, Published by Zondervans, Grand Rapids, MI, 1988, Page 587
7. Gary Don McElhany, "The South Aflame: A History of the Assemblies of God in the Gulf Region, 1901-1940," Ph.D. dissertation, Mississippi State University, 1996, 96.
8. J. Roswell Flower, "History of the Assemblies of God," (duplicated paper prepared for instructional purposes at Central Bible Institute, Springfield, MO, [1950], 17.
9. Grant Wacker, *Heaven Below: Early Pentecostals and American Culture* Cambridge, MA:Harvard University Press, 2001, 28.
10. Minutes of the General Presbytery, 1939, 2.
11. Mack M. Pinson, to J. Roswell Flower, 10 January 1951. Pinson file, FPHC.
12. *"Hot Springs Assembly, God's Glory Present*, Word Witness 10:4 (April 20, 1914).
13. Bishop Ithiel C. Clemmons, *Bishop C.H. Mason and the Roots of the Church of God in Christ,* Publisher: Pneuma Life Publishing, Bakersfield, California, 93389, Page 71.
14. Hawke, D.F., (1961), *In the Midst of a Revolution*, University of Pennsylvania Publisher.
15. James Delk, *He Made Millions Happy* (Hopkinsville, KY:Privately Published, 1950).
16. James Courts, *The History and Life Work of Bishop C.H. Mason*, Privately Published: Memphis, TN, 1919, Page 32.
17. Deposition of C.H. Mason taken April 27, 1908, case #14770, Chancery Court of Shelby County, Tennessee, Frank Avant vs. C.H. Mason, pp. 97-98.
18. Calvin S. Mc Bride, *Walking Into A New Spirituality*, Publisher iUniverse, Lincoln, Nebraska, 2007, Page, 117.

19. Gary Don McElhany, *"The South Aflame: A History of the Assemblies of God in the Gulf Region, 1901-1940,"* Ph.D. dissertation, Mississippi State University, 1996, 96.

20. J. Roswell Flower, to Mack M. Pinson, 4 January 1950. Pinson file, FPHC.

21. J. Roswell Flower, to Mack M. Pinson, 4 January 1950. Pinson file, FPHC.

22. "Fanatical Worship of Negroes Going on at Sanctified Church" article published in the *Commercial Appeal* newspaper in Memphis, Tennessee, Wednesday, May 22, 1907, pp. 5.

23. James Courts, *The History and Life Work of Bishop C.H. Mason*, Privately Published: Memphis, TN, 1919, Page 32.

24. Ibid. Page 32

25. James Delk, *He Made Millions Happy* (Hopkinsville, KY:Privately Published, 1950), Page 7.

26. Ibid. Page 8.

27. Ibid. Page 13.

28. James L. Delk, *Philosophy and Democracy*, Hopkinsville, KY: Privately Published, 1945, Page 8.

29. Ibid. Page 12.

30. Elijah L. Hill, *Women Come Alive*, Arlington, Texas, P.O. Box 181937, (Independently Published), May, 2005, Page 28.

31. Elijah L. Hill, *Women Come Alive*, Arlington, Texas, P.O. Box 181937, (Independently Published), May, 2005, Page 29.

32. Ibid. Page 31

33. Ibid. Page 32

34. Elijah Hill, *The Azusa Revival, Wrapped in Swaddling Clothes, lying in a Manger Centennial Edition.* 2006 Independently Published, Page 25.

35. Elijah L. Hill, *Women Come Alive*, Arlington, Texas, P.O. Box 181937, (Independently Published), May, 2005, Page 34.

36. Charles H. Pleas, *Fifty Years of Achievement: Church of God in Christ* Privately Published: Kansas City, KS, 1955, Page 48.

37. Jessie Carney Smith (Editor), *Notable Black American Women*, Cengage Gale Publisher, 1991, Page 723.

38. Ibid. Page 91

39. Ibid. Page 723

40. Ross, Owen. "Mary McLeod Bethune and the National Youth Administration: A Case Study of Power Relationships in the Black Cabinet of Franklin D. Roosevelt.", *Journal of Negro History* 60 (January 1975): 1-28.

41. Elijah L. Hill, *Women Come Alive*, Arlington, Texas, P.O. Box 181937, (Independently Published), May, 2005, Page 160.

42. Paula F. Pfeffer, *A. Philip Randolph, Pioneer of the Civil Rights Movement*, Baton Rouge: Louisiana State University Press, 8.

43. U.S. War Department & Federal Bureau of Investigation Files, Charles H. Mason Files Investigation Violating the Espionage Act.

44. Theron F. Schlabach & Richard T. Hughes. (1987). *Proclaim Peace: Christian Pacifism from Unexpected Quarters.* Illinois: University of Illinois Press. Page 3.

Chapter 6—Struggles and Accomplishments during World War I and World War II

April 6, 1917, was the beginning of World War I (WWI). The institution of the first draft in the United States called (Selective Service Act of 1917) had a major impact on American society. President Thomas Woodrow Wilson (the 28th president of the United States) had just been re-elected for a second term. It was interesting to note that the President maintained a neutral policy about America entering WWI, since the war had raged in Europe from 1914 without America's participation. The German nation began to attack American civilian ships forcing the hand of President Woodrow Wilson to get involved in World War I. Even then, he reluctantly requested the United States Congress to issue a declaration of war against Germany. Hundreds of thousands of young men went overseas to fight. The death toll began to climb to a devastating point.

There were circumstances and specific actions that led to the success of Bishop Charles Mason relating to his First Amendment rights regarding the Freedom of Religion in the Constitution of the United States. In 1917, Bishop Charles Harrison Mason sends a telegram to President Wilson surrounding negotiations surrounding his organization's civil liberties as Christians. Mason's reason was to maintain their religious freedom by choosing to be conscientious objectors while the country was at war. The Church of God in Christ faced seemingly insurmountable harassment, persecution, and criminal prosecution from the government for the next three years because of making this request.

One important legal issue that scholars continue to debate is the First Congress' original meaning of the First Amendment of the Free Exercise Clause.[1] It is of importance to note that historically, America has had great challenges during wartime regarding constitutional laws surrounding the First Amendment.

The Triumph of the Black Church

In 1917, President Woodrow Wilson after Bishop
Charles H. Mason had sent him a telegraph the
President invited Bishop Mason to the White House
to discuss his Church of God in Christ exemption
from World War I military service

The United States Selective Service Act 1917, the Church
Of God in Christ was the first religious group to request
exemption from the military service during World War I

Where there has been a violation of common citizens' rights when Congress created the Sedition Act of 1918.[2] During every national wartime from the American Revolution of 1776 to President George W. Bush's famous War on Terrorism. Past governmental regulations manipulated the censorship of America's Freedom of Speech in the name of protecting America's national security.[3]

It is important to uphold the purity of the guarantees of the First Amendment. True democracy must not rest upon the rule of men, but upon the rule of our constitutional law.[4] Therefore, it is upon this premise called the Church-State Law that the scholar Tamm (1999) argues that, "The opening words of the First Amendment to the U. S. Constitution, preceding even the great freedoms of speech, press, and assembly, grant Freedom of Religion. Congress shall make no law disrespecting an establishment of religion, or prohibiting the free exercise thereof."[5]

The Selective Service Act meant that male citizens over the age of eighteen had to volunteer to enlist in the military. In 1917, the scholars Schlabach & Hughes described President Wilson's statement regarding exemptions under religious liberties in time of war, President Wilson stated, "Members of a well-recognized religious sect or organization that had a creed prohibiting war service were eligible, but they still had to perform noncombatant military service."[6]

The Federal Bureau of Investigation (FBI) files of 1918 cite that Bishop Charles Harrison Mason sent a telegram to the president of the United States in 1917 to negotiate concerning his organization's tenets relating to their religious liberties. The files further revealed that Mason did meet with the War Department, and declared that the shedding of blood was against the religion of the Churches of God in Christ. After this meeting in Washington D. C., Bishop Mason's request received approval by the president's War Department.[7]

In 1918, The FBI confiscated in Beaumont, Texas this original circular issued by Bishop Charles Harrison Mason to Church of God in Christ members to give to the Selective Service boards in their community to inform that government they were conscious Objectors after President Woodrow Wilson's War Department gave the Church of God in Christ this exemption after Mason's meeting in Washington, D.C.

The Churches of God in Christ drew up a statement and gave it to their members to submit to the local Selective Service boards. It was in Lexington, Mississippi, 1918 that the local officials became insulted and upset that Negros coming from local cotton plantations would tell them that they did not have to participate in the draft because of their religious liberties.

The clerk of the court contacted the FBI with false allegations that Bishop Charles Mason was leading Negros in the South to be deserters of the Selective Service Act and to rebel against the government. As a result, Bishop Mason was arrested and placed in a Lexington jail, then sent to federal prison and booked for allegedly committing treason against the United States Government under the Sedition Act of 1918.[8]

The grand jury trial of Bishop Charles Harrison Mason took place in Paris, Texas, 1919, but the judge threw out the Federal government's case of treason because Congress later rescinded the Seditious Act of 1918 as being unconstitutional. They agreed that it was a mistake, since it violated the Constitution of the United States rule regarding freedom of religion, and the Constitution of the United States clearly stated that, "Congress could make no law in conflict or opposing the of religious freedom of Americans.[11]

Bishop Charles Harrison Mason was a true early twentieth century change leader. He implemented an innovative approach in standing upon his First Amendment Constitutional right under Freedom of Religion during Jim Crow laws in America. At this time, it was unpopular for African Americans to make a stand for their religious beliefs. Mason realized that God had created all men with equality of human rights regardless of race or the color of their skin. By holding to this position, blacks were easily under threat of death for their views. Furthermore, on page, ten of the 1917, Church of God in Christ Manual entitled, *A Brief Historical and Doctrinal Statement and Rules for Government of the Church Of God In Christ*.

¶ POLITICAL GOVERNMENTS

We believe that governments are God-given institutions for the benefit of mankind. We admonish and exhort our members to honor magistrates and the powers that be, to respect and obey the civil laws.

We hereby and herewith declare our loyalty to the President and the Constitution of the United tes, and pledge fidelity to the flag for which the ublic stands. But as a God-fearing, peace-loving and law-abiding people, we only claim our inheritance as American citizens, namely: To worship God according to the dictates of our own conscience.

We believe that the shedding of human blood or the taking of human life to be contrary to the teachings of our Lord and Saviour, and as a body we are averse to war in all its various forms.

This faith of the Church of God in Christ was adopted by its General Assembly in 1895, forbidding its members to take up arms or to shed human blood in any form.

We herewith offer our services to the President for any service that will not conflict with our conscientious scruples in this respect, with love to all, with malice toward none, and with due respect to all who differ from us in our interpretation of the Scriptures.

10

In 1918, the FBI confiscated this document from Church of God in Christ 1917 Manuel that stated that their beliefs were based upon the Constitution of the United States.

The founding fathers of the Church of God in Christ organization acknowledged clearly their loyalty to the Constitution of the United States, the President, the flag rather than the conspiracy and lies that the federal government fabricated it states:

"We hereby and herewith declare our loyalty to the President and the Constitution of the United States, and pledge fidelity to the flag for which the public stands. But as a God-fearing, peace-loving and law-abiding people, we only claim our inheritance as American citizens, namely: To worship God according to the dictates of our own conscience. We believe that the shedding of human blood or the taking of human life to be contrary to the teachings of our Lord and Savior, and as a Body, we are opposed to war in all its various forms.

"This faith of the Church of God in Christ was adopted by its General Assembly in 1895, forbidding its members to take up arms or to shed human blood in any form.

"We herewith offer our services to the President for any service that will not conflict with our conscientious scruples in this respect, with love to all, with malice toward none, and with due respect to all who differ from us in our interpretation of the Scriptures."[13]

This document found in the Federal Bureau of Investigations files in 1918 confirms the fact the Bishop Charles Harrison Mason was conscious of the Constitution of the United States of America as the bases of his argument relating to religious liberties in America. In the first paragraph he quotes that, his organization's tenets pledges loyalty to the President, the Constitution of the United States, and the flag. This removes all doubt that Bishop Mason only approached the President without knowledge of his Constitutional right as a citizen of the United States under the First Amendment Freedom of Religion. It was also clear in the Church of God in Christ tenets relating to governments that he states in the latter half of the first paragraph that we only claim our American citizenship under bases of our right to worship God according to our conscious.

This proves when the Church of God in Christ was originally founded in 1895 one year prior to Plessy vs. Ferguson, that the Constitution of the United States of America was the bases, and foundation of this above mentioned passage. They mentioned the legal document (The Constitution of the United States) in Washington, D.C., which supported their religious beliefs as the bases of their religious civil liberties in America. This also proves that the founding fathers of the Church of God in Christ understood that their religious faith was grounded civilly and scripturally, and in alignment with the Founding Fathers of the United States of America when it was written in 1776. Many historians viewed Bishop Charles Harrison Mason as just a gospel preacher and revivalist in America overlooking that fact that he was an all-around churchman and religious leader. Whose intellectual thoughts transcended just religion, but was inclusive of how religious thought, social, and political powers could interact cohesively together without conflict. Only on the bases of claiming American citizenship as the foundation to uphold, their right to worship the God of heaven based upon their own conscious and not the dictates of the federal governments criteria crystallizing what the First Amendment of the Constitution states, "Congress shall make no law in conflict of ones religion in America."

In summer of 1917, after Bishop C.H. Mason's telegram President Woodrow Wilson sent Bishop Mason the rules and requirements for being a religious conscientious objector and qualifications for a religious sect along with an invitation to come to Washington to visit him.

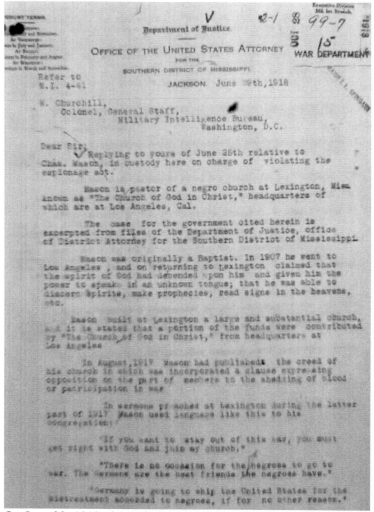

On June 29, 1918, the United States District Attorney office writes a letter to the FBI surrounding the details of Charles H. Mason's trial here are the actuals details.

Bishop Mason had wisely requested permission, ahead of time, to refrain from his organizations participation in World War I, making sure his organization was in line with the government and yet not violating the Holy Scriptures. He later met with members of the War Department Board and finalized the last request of these governmental requirements. The requirements outlined from the Bureau of Investigation were: (1) that members of his organization had to sign a registry demonstrating they were members of the Church of God in Christ and (2) send the list back to the President (3) They had to have religious tenets in place stating their conscientious objector position within their religious institution.[14]

In spite of all of his efforts to be in compliance with the government, copies of COGIC's Doctrinal Statements were published throughout the country and the FBI used them to attempt to indict Bishop Mason and the Church of God in Christ for its religious beliefs. The following year Mason was arrested and a conspiracy was developed within the FBI files stating that Mason was, "a Pro-German who was influencing his members not to go to war because he was on the side of the German empire."

One of the approaches the FBI used ground their conspiracy theory was that Mason had many white followers and leaders. They identified that two of them were of German ethnicity, so the government tried to use this to give strength to this conspiracy theory. Even though all European whites that came from Europe were of all ethnic backgrounds what area of Europe they came from like, Germany, Russia, French, Yugoslavian, etc. If the United States government went out and rounded up all Americans that had German descent they would had many significant citizens in America, this would have created a situation like what happened with the Chinese and Japanese placing them all in concentration camps during WWII. Yet, the United States government only harassed white brothers that had German descent that choose to follow an African American leader during Jim Crow this gave them an opportunity to justify trying to threaten them through harassment tactics from being a part of the African American Church of God in Christ Pentecostal denomination.

Another reason the government tried to use as evidence was a sermon Bishop Mason had delivered about the topic of WWI on June 23, 1918, a year after America entered the war. The title was "The Kaiser in Light of the Scriptures!"[15] In this message, Mason told the people not to look to the power of the United States, England, France, or Germany, but to trust in God. He was concerned with the war from the respect that God had revealed to him the spiritual and scriptural meaning of World War I. Bishop Mason felt that WWI would cause millions of souls in military service to be hurled into judgment without having an opportunity to give their life to Christ. He believed that Christians should lend their support to the government though financially supporting through bonds, but that Christians should be committed to being pacifists based upon their religious beliefs.

In Mason's message, he revealed to the people that there were prophetic Old Testament passages that were types of World War I, and symbolic referring to Kaiser Wilhelm II. This is why he called the title of the message, "The Kaiser in the Light of Scripture" because God had revealed to Bishop Mason through different passages of scriptures the very actions of the Kaiser who started the first World War.[16]

First Bishop Mason shared how Kaiser Wilhelm II of Germany went into the temple to pray, but came out to declare war. He shared a series of Scripture about how an individual should act who knows God that starting a war after they pray is not a godly spirit.

Mason shared these Scriptures found in Roman 14:17; I Timothy 2:1–2; and I Timothy 2:8; that people would observe that wrath against another people was not from God, so Professor Court's documented detail facts on this sermon in his book, which says:

"In I Timothy 2:8, the Apostle again says, *'I will therefore that men pray everywhere, lifting up holy*

The Triumph of the Black Church

1959 J.O. Patterson & Dr. King Memphis   Rally COGIC Memphis Dr. King

1968 COGIC Memphis King Last Speech   COGIC, King Family after death

1968 Lorraine Hotel Memphis   1968, Moments after King Slaying

August 28, 1963, March on Washington, 250,000 attend

hands, without wrath or doubting.' The wrathful
attitude of the Kaiser's prayer, with the purpose to
work wrath was a vain prayer in which he had not
the spirit of Christ or the authority of the Scriptures.
Thus, the prayer of the Kaiser was unscriptural."

Next Mason described a comparative analysis of the actions
and strategic decisions of Kaiser Wilhelm II the emperor of
Germany step-by-step as World War I enfolded using the Scripture
text of Habakkuk 2:5–8 as his foundation. Bishop Mason referred
to various passages to demonstrate that Biblical passages were
relevant to current world events in the news.[17]
Bishop Mason's goal was to increase people's awareness
that the prophets of old already foresaw some current events
hidden thousands of years before through typology in God's Holy
Word that was relevant and spoke to current dilemmas confronted
within the World War I, by the human race. Here are some of the
Scriptures that Mason referenced to reveal biblical symbolic
comparisons of Kasier of Germany in 1918.

"Quoting Habakkuk 2:5, *'He is a proud man,
neither keepeth at home, he enlargeth his desire as
hell, and is as death, cannot be satisfied, but
gathereth unto him all nations and heapeth unto
him all people.'* The Kaiser's ambition was to rule
the world and the spirit of militarism possessed him.
This portion of portion of Old Testament passage
accurately describes his character and his action
during WWI. He does not want to keep at home,
but is reaching out hands dripping with the blood of
innocent children and defenseless women sent to a
sudden death. The Kaiser used the barbarous
method of submarine warfare, which is out of
harmony with all the laws of humanity, and fair
play violating of all the principles of civilized
warfare. The German Kaiser is seemingly

1915, Kaiser Wilhelm II Emperor of Germany
Bishop Charles H. Mason prophesied about he
would lost World War I, it lost five days later

attempting to gather to himself all nations and to rule all peoples. Not satisfied with the rape of Belgium, he has overthrown the governments of Romania and Montenegro, and through hypocrisy and deceit he betrayed Russia into a disgraceful peace."[18]

In Professor, Court's book went deeply into the details revealing Mason's prophesy, he stated:

"Quoting Habakkuk 2:6–8, *'shall not all these take up a parable against him, and a taunting proverb against him, and say Woe to him that increaseth that which is not his, shall they not rise up suddenly? That shall bite thee, and awake that shall vex thee? Because thou hast spoiled thee because of men's blood, and for the violence of the land of the city and all that dwell therein.'* Mason declared that if anyone is building hopes on the victories of the Kaiser in the present war, their hopes eventually would be in vain. Although, he may suddenly conquer nations and devastated cities, in the end he hast to meet God's conditions. Mason prophesied based upon these passages his outcome that the remnant of the Germans left from the devastation of war will rise up against him (the Kaiser) and cry, "Woe unto thee because thou hast spoiled many nations, the people shall spoil thee."[19]

This is exactly how it happened. Kaiser Wilhelm II's own military refused to fight for him, and his main generals asked him to step down from power. This was a big step for the German people, because the Kaiser was not only the ruler of the German country, but he was from a royal bloodline. Kaiser Wilhelm II was a royal prince, his father, grandfather, and great-grandfather for generations had ruled the throne of Germany, and now he had to give an official Statement of Abdication on November 28, 1918. This Statement of Abdication declared that Kaiser Wilhelm II had no say in the throne of Germany or the military. The Kaiser, after this, fled the country afraid of his outcome just as Mason had foretold through biblical scriptures.

Mason's sermon takes place in Memphis, Tennessee on June 23, 1918, and five days later on June 28, 1918, the famous signing of Treaty of Versailles takes place as a cease-fire for WWI. Bishop Charles Mason prophesied the downfall of Kaiser Wilhelm II of Germany before it ever happened through this message, "The Kaiser in the Light of Scripture."

When President Woodrow Wilson did implement the Selective Service Act in America in 1917, this position had a great impact on many Christians who refuse the draft, based upon their religious faith. Nationally, as many whites as blacks followed the conscientious objector stance and other Holiness and Pentecostal organizations all over America followed suit agreeing with Bishop Charles Harrison Mason.

The passing of the Sedition Act forbade Americans to use disloyal, profane, scurrilous, or abusive language about the United States government or flag, or armed forces during war. The Sedition Act made it a crime to utter, print, write, or publish any disloyal, profane, scurrilous, or abusive language about the United States Government."[22]

President Wilson's paranoia had translated into overstepping even the power of the Constitution of the United States of America. Actually, this law was the first implemented by an American President in the name of wartime that abused the constitutional rights of the American citizens.

This Act was a direct violation of The First Amendment to the Constitution of the United States Freedom of Speech, which states in part, "Congress shall make no law abridging the freedom of speech, or the press."

36

THE KAISER IN THE LIGHT OF THE SCRIPTURES.

Sermon Preached By Elder C. H. Mason, Memphis, Tenn., June 23, 1918—(By Elder Wm. B. Holt, Secretary to General Overseer).

The baptismal sermon preached by Elder C. H. Mason, General Overseer of the Church of God in Christ, to a vast throng that gathered to witness the baptismal ceremonies at North Memphis.

The Overseer was led to speak of the German Kaiser in the light of the scriptures, basing his remarks on the vision of the prophet as recorded in the second chapter of Habakkuk—Hab. 2;2, "The Lord answered me and said, 'Write the vision and make it plain.''

They tell me, the Kaiser went into prayer and came out and lifted up his hands and prayed, and afterwords declared war.

Let us see, what did he pray and for what did he pray? Surely he did not pray thy Kingdom Come, because the Kingdom of God is righteousness, peace and joy in the Holy Ghost.—Rom.14:17.

If he had been praying for peace he would not have declared war.

The Apostle Paul declared in 1 Tim. 2:1-2, I exhort therefore that, first of all, supplications, prayers, intercessions and giving of thanks be made for all men—for kings and for all who are in authority—that we may lead a quite and peaceful life in all Godliness and honesty. If he had the spirit of this prayer he himself would have endeavored to live a peaceful life.

In 1 Tem. 2:8, the apostle again says, I will therefore that men pray everywhere, lifting up holy hands, with-

On June 23, 1918, Bishop Mason preached this sermon prophesying the Kaiser of Germany would lost World War I here is the sermon

It was very easy for the President to get the law passed because it was an amendment to an earlier law, the Espionage Act, which dealt with only sharing of information with other enemy countries. The American government used the Sedition Act of 1918; to empower the Federal Bureau of Investigation secretly collected counterintelligence against American citizens based upon the Sedition Act making it a crime of treason against the United States. The government was so paranoid of individuals speaking against the war if a religious group communicated to their members that they were consciousness objectors. The government would falsely accuse them that they spoke against the war by sending communication to their members. Many were imprisoned falsely religious individuals for many years behind the government's misuse of the Sedition Act.

Three years later Congress repealed this law because of its unconstitutional nature, which had made free speech illegal in America. Many American citizens that were conscientious objectors because of their religious beliefs were imprisoned and executed for their religious beliefs.[23]

This first instance of using war as a scare tactic to influence the Congress of the United States is something historically that needs to be monitored, because former Presidents are known after Wilson to do things in the name of protecting the peace of America but violating the constitutional rights of its citizens. When the terrorist attacks occurred in America in 2001, and the destroying of New York Twin Towers, President George W. Bush asked for to implement a law was a violation of American's civil liberties.

The Homeland Security Act had certain amendments violated American citizen's privacy rights under the name of protecting the United States. As time went on the American Press began to challenge President Bush, and the policies that gave the Homeland Security this right to violate citizen's rights.

President Wilson found out about Bishop Charles Mason's influence with thousands of whites and blacks refusing to join the selective service within the Church of God in Christ and other Pentecostal organizations followed suit with Mason's organization.

President Wilson approved the opening of FBI file against Bishop Mason to find out what had caused him to have such great influence in a white racist society that caused thousands of whites to follow Mason's conscientious objector position.[24]

In addition to Mason's position on pacifism, this meant that as a Christian it was against their religion to take human life, of which the Constitution of the United States supported Mason's position under freedom of religion. Bishop Charles Mason and other Christian groups spoke out surrounding their Christian beliefs about objecting to participate in WWI. What is so ironic is the fact that President Wilson's religious background was a pacifist. He was opposed to war, and he won re-election of the presidency on his second term based on the premise that he would not take the country to war.

Bishop Charles Mason's sermon mentioned nothing against the United States Government, and he complimented President Wilson for issuing a national Proclamation for the American People to fast and pray before going to war. He admired the President for choosing to do as godly biblical rulers and kings did by calling the people together to seek God's face on the matter of going into battle. Mason even complimented the President; sharing with the members of his organization how he was in harmony with the Scriptures.

The United States Government issued Liberty Bonds in WWI, in order for the American public to assist the government in financing the war. Contradictory to the FBI files Bishop Mason personally supported the war effort in America by loaning $3000 in Liberty Bonds. In the same sermon he makes it known that he supports the war effort, and was in the favor of the success of the Allied Troops in Europe. In Professor Court's book, he reveals Mason's perspective on his organization's financial support of the war, which disproved even more the conspiracy theory the FBI, Professor Courts address this topic in his biography of Bishop C.H. Mason, he wrote:

IS IT RIGHT TO BUY LIBERTY BONDS? YES.

What does it mean to buy Liberty Bonds?

It means to loan to your Government a certain amount of money.

What says the Scriptures?

Jesus said in Matthew 5:42: "Give to him that asketh thee, and from them that would borrow of thee turn not thou away."

Brethren, we are to live by every word of God, Matthew 4:4.

Our Government is asking us for a loan and we are in no violation of God's word in granting it, and not only to loan, but loan, hoping for no gain—Luke, 6:35.

ELDER C. H. MASON,
General Overseer of the Church of God in Christ.

In 1919, Statement put out by Bishop C.H. Mason about supporting the this contradicted the conspiracy theory in court of the FBI

"Answering the question that has been asked him many times, namely, is it right to buy Liberty Bonds, his (Bishop Mason's) reply was, "Yes! Yes!" And he proceeded to define the Liberty Bonds. What does it mean to buy Liberty Bonds? It means to lend your country a certain amount of money. What says the Scripture? Matthew 5:42, *Give to him that asketh thee, and from them that borrow of thee turn not away. Brethren, we are living by every word of God* (Matthew 4:4). "Our government is asking for a loan, and we are in no violation of God's word in granting it, and not only to loan, but loan hoping for nothing to gain (St. Luke 6:35). I have loaned the government, and have succeeded in raising for the help of the government more than three thousand dollars, in taking out bonds, and as far as I am concerned, the spiritual injunction stands. I have loaned, hoping for nothing in return."[27]

Despite Bishop Mason's effort to support the war financially and having obtained the President's approval, an arrest was made and he was arrested and tried for treason against the U.S. Government. In the book, *The Biography of Bishop Charles Harrison Mason,* Mason shares with the courts how the final trial turns out for him:

"In 1918 I was called to appear before the judge of the Kangaroo Court in Paris, Texas. The presiding officers looked at me and laid down his books, and said, "You all may try him; I will not have anything to do with him." I will give God all the glory Amen."[28]

The judge in Paris, Texas recognized who Mason was that praying man with a reputation of God's power being demonstrated, and the judge laid down his books and told the United States District Attorney you may try him I will not having anything to do with him. The power of God intervened on Mason's behalf supernaturally God would not allow man or the United States government to falsely accuse him. Bishop C.H. Mason walked in a supernatural anointing in his pray life, and the power of God delivered him from the power of human corrupt judicial systems in America during the height of Jim Crow in America.

The five categories that Bishop Mason made a major historical impact on were: (1) Religion in America; (2) Jim Crowism in America Race Relations in America (3) His influence of Military's Conscious Objector principle, (4) First African American leader Speaks to Communicate about Global leaders of WWI, (5) Bishop Mason's Influence in WWII Shipyards iron distribution.

This action by the government created a very turbulent year; in 1918. Persecutions were unleashed as a windstorm of political power came to crush this young God-given movement by attacking the leader with false and frivolous conspiracies in an attempt to put him in prison and executed if found guilty of Treason against the United States. This was nothing short of attempting to break the momentum of what was to become the largest African American Pentecostal organization in the world.

One of many victims was Rev. Jesse Payne, a Church of God in Christ preacher from Blytheville, Arkansas an angry white mob tarred and feathered him publicly. The *Memphis Commercial Appeal* headlines were, "Negro Preacher Tarred." The report read:

> "Pastor of the colored holy roller church in the southeast suburbs of this city, was given a coat of tar and feathers last night as a result of alleged seditious remarks for some months concerning the President, the war and a white man's war. Earlier in the evening the preacher is alleged to have said something about the Kaiser being as good a man as

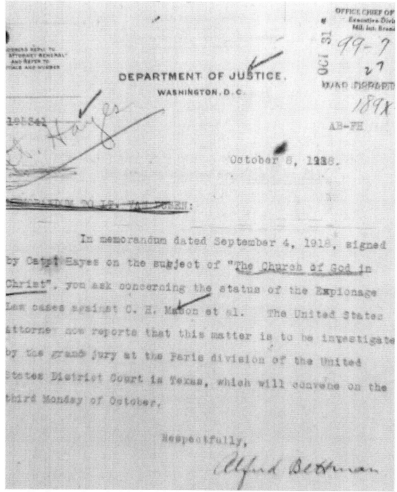

In September 4, 1918, this is a memorandum taken from the FBI files documenting their notes from the Department of Justice in Washington, D.C., that the C.H. Mason trial against the United States Attorney General's office. It stated the court case would be held in Paris, Texas here is the actual document.

the President, and that the Kaiser did not require his people to buy bonds. Someone then landed a solar plexus on him sending him into the ditch; from which he got up running.

"After the tarring and feathering, Payne repeated the soldier's oath, and promised to talk Liberty Bonds and Red Cross to the end of his life and the end of the war. It is said his flock has shown no interest in the war work, while the negroes of other churches have been most liberal; $2000 having been subscribed by the Methodist and the Baptist churches Sunday night. This church is circulating literature which he says was sent to him by a brother preacher in Memphis, showing from Bible quotations that it is not right for Christians to fight. The literature is scattered and broadcast over the country."[45]

The discriminatory perception of white America could not accept the fact that this religious movement had so influence on both white and black Americans. With the founder being a black man, they felt insulted that thousands of Americans was listening to Mason's voice over theirs. As Herod, the King who represented the government in Christ's day and who wanted to destroy the plan of God to facilitate his own fleshly envy, so it was with the U.S. government in 1918. These incidents are but a few of the violent acts against the Church of God in Christ that occurred in 1918:

> 1. Blytheville, Arkansas—Elder Payne tarred, feathered, and jailed for preaching on the conscientious objector stance from the pulpit
> 2. Elder Mangrum of N.E. Michigan, the father of Supervisor Mary Johnson, was fatally shot
> 3. Mother Lizzie Robinson was jailed for spreading the gospel

4. Bishop Mason was investigated by the FBI as a traitor of the U.S. government, and tried for treason against the United States

5. Bishop Mason was physically knocked down while being arrested by a police officer

6. Mason was arrested in Lexington, Mississippi, and placed in a county jail for several days

7. Mason was barred by the judge from entering the state of Mississippi for a year

8. Mason was booked, and then transferred to federal prison in Jackson, Mississippi

9. Mason was arrested in Paris, Texas, then placed in jail again

10. Mason was given trial dates for the district courts of Jackson, Mississippi, and Paris, Texas

11. The church had to come up with approximately $5000 to post bond during the different times. Mason was arrested and jailed in various states, in order to regain Mason's freedom prior to awaiting his trial.[46]

On December 14, 1921, at the 14th Holy Convocation in Memphis, Tennessee, the trading board was put into place to locate a new plot of ground to build a new national temple, since Bishop Mason's church was filled to the overflow when they held their National Holy Convocation in Memphis, TN. The National Elder's Council authorized a trading board committee to implement the planning and negotiations for a new facility appointing these ministers to serve on that board: W.M. Roberts; H.L. Kirvine; I.S. Stafford; E.M. Page; J.E. Bryant; and Elder W.M.B. Holt. They located the property near Fifth Street where the old Freeman's Hospital was located in Memphis, Tennessee, and the deal closed with a land contract at $40,000 to purchase the property. The owners allowed the Church of God in Christ to pay them $10,000 annually, until the $40,000 balance was paid in full.

Bishop Mason designated the month of January (in 1922) as the National Churches General Fund Day to raise the money for the first proposed new national temple and to purchase the land. He requested that each member of the Church of God in Christ give one dollar on that designated day to raise the funds to make the purchase the land to fulfill the land contract.[47]

In 1925, four years later the grand opening of the Old Tabernacle building was, dedicated moving the national meeting from Bishop Mason's church at 392 South Wellington Street, and the conducting of Church of God in Christ national Holy Convocation services were hosted at this new national tabernacle on 958 South 5th Street. Bishop Mason's old church had been the host facility for the national Holy Convocation meetings for sixteen years since 1907. Mason's church was a brick structure that was 40 by 100 feet with a balcony, dining room, kitchen, two rest rooms, and a pastor's study. God revealed to Bishop C. H. Mason that the Holy Convocation would become so filled to capacity no facility could hold the people. Many times revival services were held outside.[48] There were many who attended the Holy Convocation to receive their healing, even on the outside of the Old Tabernacle's sanctuary.

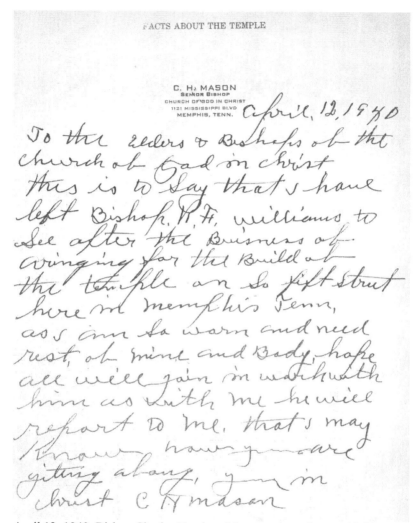

FACTS ABOUT THE TEMPLE

C. H. MASON
SENIOR BISHOP
CHURCH OF GOD IN CHRIST
1121 MISSISSIPPI BLVD
MEMPHIS, TENN.

April 12, 1940, Bishop Charles Harrison Mason writes a letter with his own Hand writing to inform the church that he has left Bishop Riley F. Williams in charge of the building of Mason Temple their future World Headquarters. That Bishop Williams would report to him because he was feeling worn in his body, and he personally signed the letter.

It was in 1937 that the worst tragedy occurred when the Old Temple burned to the ground in 1925. It was a blessing that not one life was lost. Paperwork and historical documents that told many details of the church's history were lost.

One of the first five men appointed as a bishop was Riley F. Williams who was one of the young aggressive and dynamic preachers that followed the COGIC organization. Bishop Williams became the overseer of Alabama and Ohio, and in 1934, he hired Pastor U.E. Miller to be his superintendent of construction. Bishop Williams hired him to implement and oversee his vision at his jurisdictional headquarters in Cleveland, Ohio. Bishop Williams headquarters in Cleveland, Ohio was to become the first largest local Church of God in Christ structure built from the ground up in the mid 1930's.[49]

Bishop Riley F. Williams, who originally started his ministry in Louisiana, had conducted several revivals throughout the state of Louisiana. At one of these revivals, U.E. Miller gave his life to Christ him and his future wife Delphia Bell whom Miller married on June 17, 1917. Bishop Miller was born October 16, 1893, in Elmo, Louisiana, to Ellis and Roslyn Miller. Bishop Williams led him to the Lord, and as a result, their close friendship came about. Bishop Williams realized U.E. Miller had a strong background in educational training in the field of construction, and he recognized his amazing ability as an artisan and hired him on as a construction supervisor to construct the Williams Temple in Ohio. When this amazing structure was finished, it was valued at $65,000. The newspapers in Cleveland, Ohio, covered the story giving it national attention. And Bishop Mason was overjoyed to learn that this great accomplishment was the work of one of his sons in the ministry.[50] This inspired Bishop Mason appoint U.E. Miller as the national secretary of the national church in 1934. The national secretary of the Church of God in Christ was a white brother named William Holt from 1907-1934, and Miller was the first African America to hold that national office. Bishop U.E. Miller kept that coveted office until 1963. Bishop Mason soon asked Miller to design him a temple that was similar to the White House.

The location of the National Holy Convocations took place at 5th Street for over twelve years after it burned down; therefore, Bishop Mason had to return to his main church for the National Convocation meetings on Wellington Street because of the recent fire that destroyed the Old Tabernacle in 1937. It was around this time that Bishop Mason needed someone to oversee his next national building project. Bishop Riley F. Williams was his choice for the job because Bishop Riley F. Williams had accomplish what no one else had to date to build a local jurisdictional temple as large as the one he had built in Cleveland, Ohio.[51]

The nation had just emerged from the Great Depression. Directly after that America enter into WWII with an act of force after the bombing of Pearl Harbor in December 1941. It was during this time that Mason undertook one of the most progressive construction visions of the Church of God in Christ organization within the first half of the Twentieth Century. This next building was to become one of the largest facilities built and owned by African Americans in the United States. Mason dared to expand his national building program despite even the country's financial recession. In addition to America's financial situation, there was only $2900 available in the national treasurer's account. Bishop Williams was surprised at Bishop Charles Harrison Mason's decision to build during this time when peoples finance was at its lowest after the Great Depression. While Mason was in California hosting a camp meeting ministering to the saints, Mason spoke by phone to Bishop Williams to proceed, stating, "I will call for the finances from the people to meet the obligation of the project."[52] He had no doubt that the money would come for such a grand and expansive project. Mason realized that God had given him the vision, and the Lord would provide the necessary provisions.

Bishop Riley F. Williams felt the vigorous optimism of his leader, so he came up with a creative way to multiply the initial resources of the national church from $2900 to $6900.

In 1940, Bishop Riley F. Williams was appointed
by Bishop Mason to build Mason Temple which
would end up being the largest facility built from
the ground up owned by African Americans

1940, H. Taylor, Architect for Mason Temple

The first thing that Bishop Riley Williams did was to double the amount of money in the national church's treasury, so he went to a bank and asked for a loan that doubled the amount existing in the treasury. Bishop Mason's credit and influence in the Memphis community enabled Williams to take out two small loans of $2000 from two banks. Individuals in the white community were supportive when it came to advancing the ministry of Bishop Charles Harrison Mason. After securing these loans, Bishop Riley Williams was able to increase the initial construction capitol to $6900.[53]

As Bishop Williams proceeded to appeal to different companies regarding the construction of this large temple, white business owners were familiar with Bishop Mason, and were glad to help make his vision a reality. Bishop Mason's ministry had positively influenced the Memphis community for thirty or more years. His name was a household word among the political and business leadership of that community. Bishop Mason had appointed Bishop Louis Henry Ford to be his national public relations director. His duties was to coordinate Mason's Civic night services which involved giving the Church of God in Christ visibility with political leaders by inviting them to address the Church of God in Christ constituency during their National Convention in Memphis, TN. Bishop Louis Henry Ford was one of the strategic leaders within the Church of God in Christ organization he maintained political relationship with political leaders many times he would invite Governors, Mayors, and City Council representative to address Mason's services during the Holy Convocation. Bishop Ford would later become a Presiding Bishop of the Church of God in Christ and would be the first to invite a setting United State President Bill Clinton to visit a National African American Religious Convention in America later in the 1990's. Bishop L.H. Ford's political influence was so strong in Chicago, Illinois where he lived that later after his death he became the only African American preacher to have an interstate named after him in Chicago, Illinois called the Bishop Louis Henry Ford Expressway. Therefore, Williams started out his project by securing the best construction Manger he could find, U.E. Miller. He knew that securing U.E. Miller's extraordinary construction management skills to be on his team would be essential for the national project's success.[54]

In addition, to increasing the national church's funds, Bishop Williams needed to hire an architect to design the details of the edifice. However, this would have put them over budget, so he and Miller agreed to sacrifice and work without any compensation, since the funds for the national building project were limited. He hired Elder W. H. Taylor, a professional architect, to design this new facility to Bishop Mason's visionary specifications. The construction team members met with Bishop Mason to envision his design for this great temple of worship. They made the final decision that the building material would be limestone brick.[55]

Bishop Mason wanted those entering the edifice to sense an atmosphere of divine beauty; so he requested that the front entrance face west. This way the sun's rays would highlight the front entrance during setting of the sun. He envisioned that many in the future would enter at this point of the entrance for years to come. The construction team agreed that the entrance steps needed to be twenty feet wide and twenty-five feet in length, to accommodate the future crowds making their way into this great temple to worship God.[56] The construction team took under advisement Mason's suggestion on how individuals would enter the future Mason Temple Church of God in Christ World Headquarters. In addition, to the main entrance, there would be two other entrances from the north and south constructed.

Bishop Mason mentioned the importance of the sun setting on the main entrance of the temple. The construction team envisioned a large lobby with high ceilings that accommodate a large overflow of about fifty to seventy-five individuals entering the main sanctuary. The main entrance to the lobby would be made of glass to allow the sun's heat and light to give off a glorious luminous effect before entering the main sanctuary of Mason Temple.[57]

1940, Bishop U. E. Miller Construction Superintendent
Who helped Bishop Riley F. Williams to build the Temple

In 1942, the cornerstone of Mason Temple in Memphis,
TN, that states Bishop R. F. Williams Building
Commissioner, U.E. Miller, Construction Supt &
H. Taylor Architect erected in 1940.

Every aspect of this project experienced many delays because of the backdrop of WWII, which had already began in Europe (September 1939). President Franklin D. Roosevelt had already begun to dialogue with the allies in Europe. As a result, America was not yet become involved with World War II, yet the President had already started the Selective Service Draft in 1940. This action was prophetic, because Pearl Harbor would be bombed one year later on December 7, 1941. This incident would solidify America's entrance into World War II having lost thousands of American lives during the Pearl Harbor bombing at the hands of the Japanese pilots. This mobilized hundreds of thousands of men to be draftees in the war, and transformed our nation's economic focus solely on the war effort.

The government utilized all scientific and industrial labor in America to convert the building industry's focus on building weapons of war, such as ships, tanks, and guns. President Roosevelt and the United States Congress realized that obtaining raw materials like steel, cooper, and aluminum would need to become a strict priority for our country. Therefore, they appointed the War Productions Board (who was given the task to implement a priority classification) to ration raw materials; this limited private industry from accessing steel and other raw materials as freely as before.

The United States' ports became shipyards that manufactured ships for the military. Many companies in the private industry converted to shipbuilding and artillery production. The shipyards produced 4,000 or more ships; which required so many raw materials that the nation had to deal with shortages in the private sector. The massive construction project of the Church of God in Christ World Headquarters had to be placed on hold since the project required steel trusses to build the temple and because many engineers were deployed to assist with the war effort. Nevertheless, God made a way and opened that door to get the trusses manufactured in time for the 1945 deadline.

Then there were times that the money did not come in at the right time to take care of needed projects, and this delayed the construction even further. Bishop Riley Williams was constantly in the government's office inquiring about the Church of God in Christ's position in the long list for steel allotments. One day when he went into the office an individual told him that the Church of God in Christ was close to the top on the list for steel allotments. Bishop Riley William had waited for 2 years for this approval.[58]

Elder James Delk discovered that the United States War Productions Board delayed Mason Temple's steel allotment, and he used his political influence in Washington, D.C., to move the request forward. Pastor James Delk a white Church of God in Christ pastor who was friends with President Franklin D. Roosevelt. He campaigned on Roosevelt's behalf during his last term in office. In 1944, Pastor Delk spoke at the Democratic National Convention on behalf of Franklin D. Roosevelt when he was chosen as the Presidential Nominee for that year. Pastor James Delk represented himself as a white pastor in the Church of God in Christ that was a part of an African American Denomination. This event was historical because Delk became the first member of the first Church of God in Christ to speak at the Democratic National Convention. This was before African Americans were allowed to vote in the South or become a part of a political party during Plessy vs. Ferguson. Here is a correspondence written to Delk regarding his invitation to speak at the Democratic National Convention:

October 14, 1944

Mr. Donald M. Lathrom,
Director,
Democratic National Committee,
Biltmore Hotel,
New York 17, New York

Dear Mr. Lathrom:

In 1940, because the white brother Pastor James Delk had so much respect for Bishop Mason he went to Washington, D.C. personally to negotiate. He finally got word to speak with the state Senator of Tennessee to see if he could get the steel released.

In 2012, the remodeled and modernized Mason Temple remodeled during Bishop Louis Henry Ford's Administration in 1993

Your letter of October 10 was forwarded to me. In reply, I have been a minister 41 years, am 57 years old, ordained in the Church of God in Christ and have my own church at Hopkinville, Kentucky, where we broadcast by remote control direct from our church.

In 1932, I ran for the Democratic nomination for the governor of the state of Missouri. I am personally acquainted with Honorable S. Truman and Honorable Alben W. Barkley and Senator Happy Chandler of Kentucky.[59]

From 1932 until December 1943, I was opposed to our President Franklin D. Roosevelt and made speeches for Herbert Hoover in 1932 and Alfred M. Landon in 1936, and did some secret work in the interest of Mr. Wendell L. Wilkie in 1940. I am happy to say that I am radically changed and none is any more enthusiastic for the Honorable Franklin D. Roosevelt and Honorable Harry S. Truman's election than I am. Anything that I can do, I stand ready to cancel my church engagements and go down the line a hundred per cent for the Fourth Term for Honorable Franklin D. Roosevelt. I believe he is the greatest man, humanly speaking, that has been born of woman, since the day of Alexander the Great.

I'll be home at Hopkinsville, Kentucky from Sunday, October 15th to Wednesday, October 18th. Any letters or telegrams can reach me direct there. After that date, my secretary will reach me immediately.

Fight on with all your might and let's elect the greatest man in the world for President and Honorable Harry S. Truman for Vice-President.

Very Sincerely Yours,

Rev. James L. Delk[60]

Pastor Delk made many attempts to start conversations with individuals in Washington, D.C. to get the steel priority for Mason Temple. He finally met with United States Senator Tom Stewart of Tennessee who was able to persuade the government to give the steel allotment to Bishop Mason's organization on Pastor Delk's behalf. A newspaper published surrounding this article on March 22, 1945, in Los Angeles, California, surrounding the Tennessee senator Tom Stewart receiving the War Department's approval of the steel allotment for the Church of God in Christ construction project here is the article:

$48,000 CHURCH IS MADE POSSIBLE BY
SENATOR OF TENNESSEE

U.S. Senator Tom Stewart, Democrat, Tennessee has made Millions Happy.

The above were the boxcar headlines in *The Neighborhood News* of Los Angeles, California, published Thursday, March 22, 1945.

The Neighborhood News is the largest Negro paper published in the West. We quote the exact words from The Neighborhood Headquarters of The Church of God in Christ, Memphis, Tennessee.

Recently Rev. Delk met Mr. Jim Erwing who is the National Chairman of the Publicity Board of the

In 1940, Pastor James Delk helps with steel from government

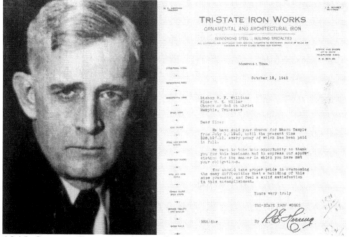

1945, Senator Stewart gets steel release from War Department

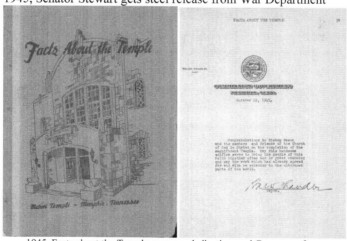

1945, Facts about the Temple program dedication, and Governor of
Tennessee acknowledging the building of Mason Temple

Church of God in Christ and as soon as definite proof was furnished him what U. S. Senator Tom Stewart did, he immediately published the great act of Mr. Stewart in securing the steel priority. This is just one of the many great things that Senator Tom Stewart in securing the steel priority. It will be remembered that Senator Stewart assisted Hon. William Jennings Bryan in the scopes trial at Dayton, Tennessee, several years ago in which they won their case. Senator Tom Stewart will never be forgotten by millions of people in America for his great achievement.

Rev. Delk, who has recently arrived in Los Angeles, California, from Hopkinsville, Kentucky, has also great praise for the Senator, and says he has presidential timber in him. Rev. Delk is conducting a series of revival meetings in the Church of God in Christ for Rev. Matthews, Pastor, church located at 488 North Mountainview Avenue. Rev. Delk is the guest of Bishop and Mrs. S. M. Crouch.

James Delk had always been a faithful member of the Church of God in Christ, and because of his love for Bishop Mason, he wanted to see his vision come to past. Pastor James Delk contacted one of the state senators of Tennessee Tom Stewart, and he had him to inquire about the steel allotment on behalf of the Church of God in Christ Church organization.[61]

The first allotment requested by Riley Williams was only for $20,000, but on October 7, 1944, the United States War Department Board approved the total $48,000 steel allotment for the final construction of Mason Temple in Memphis, Tennessee. God miraculously used James Delk to assist in the completion of Mason Temple. Pastor Delk as a white brother in the Church of God in Christ had a great admiration for the ministry of Bishop Charles Harrison Mason, because Mason never showed a difference in how he treated men of other races whether they be white or black.

Bishop Mason was able to raise around $43,000 for his construction budget. The next year (1942), the construction team received $42,069; in that year alone. The Church of God in Christ finances increased despite the financial hardships of a slow moving economy and America coming out of the Great Depression. It was difficult for individuals from day-to-day to purchase the necessities of life, but the entire national church and all its national auxiliaries stood behind the construction effort. In the next three years, the financial thrust continued, and Bishop Mason encouraged the church to support the goal of finishing the temple by 1945, the Year of Jubilee Celebration of Mason's Ministry. Mother Lizzie Robinson's Women's Department Auxiliary became a vital force in raising the total funds Bishop Mason needed. They raised close to $140,000 of the total construction budget amount of $275,676.35.[62]

Bishop Charles H. Mason witnessed phenomenal growth in the Church of God in Christ organization that he had helped to found in 1895. Bishop William J. Seymour visited the Holy Convocation of 1919 (three years before he died). When he attended this meeting, he stated that the Church of God in Christ would evolve into one of the greatest Pentecostal organizations in the world. The father of Modern Day Pentecostalism Bishop William J. Seymour pronounced that God had given his work of multicultural worship to Bishop Charles Harrison Mason. Seymour confirmed that Mason had maintained his original doctrine and faith that he had once preached to all races.

The Triumph of the Black Church

1955 Bishop L.H. Ford Emmitt Till body Chicago train station consoles his mother who were members of Ford's church in Chicago, IL the St. Paul Church of God in Christ, Ford was National Public Relations for Bishop Charles Harrison Mason when Emmitt Till's death occurred

1950, Emmitt Till a member of the Church of God in Christ he was called the sacrificial lamb of Civil Rights Movement in America his violent death started aggressive protest in America that encouraged civil protest for civil rights

1955, Bishop Louis H. Ford at the grave site of Emmitt Till giving the final burial rites with the mother and family at the grave site in Chicago, Illinois

1997, Bishop Ford is only African American preacher with Highway Naming In America because he was known by most Presidents from Truman to Clinton

On December 10, 1919, during the Church of God in Christ annual business meeting thousands of pastors and overseers throughout the United States had gathered there in Memphis, TN to witness William Seymour's last meeting with the Church of God in Christ three years before he died. The minutes stated:

"Elder W.J. Seymour of Chicago, who also was one of the founders of this great movement, came to us at this hour. How glad our hearts were made to meet him. Order of business was suspended for a few minutes to greet him. Elder Seymour then spoke of his long and wearisome trip and how glad he was to get here. He said he looked upon the Church of God in Christ to be the greatest movement on earth. Therefore, he rejoiced to stand among the greatest people on earth. He asked us to contend for the doctrine. He also repudiated even the thought of fornication in the ministry. In his conclusion, he urged that the ministry not only be fruitful but to show their fruits. Chief Apostle Mason made some very timely remarks by way of responding in the noble sayings of Elder Seymour. He concluded by singing in the spirit a song of welcome."[63]

The Church of God in Christ literally had become the pre-established foundation of Civil Rights before the Civil Rights Movement in America. In February 1995, *The Whole Truth National Newspaper* for the Church of God in Christ records these milestones for the organization and its struggles for freedom and equality among African Americans, it states:

"Emmett Till who was the sacrificial lamb of the Civil Rights Movement in America. He was a member of the Church of God in Christ. Bishop Louis Henry Ford was his pastor when his mother sent him down to Money, Mississippi, to visit his grandmother for the summer when he was beaten beyond recognition in 1955."

The account of 14-year-old Emmett Till, whose abduction and brutal beating in a later magazine stated:

> At 6:00a.m., another black youth, on his way to his grandmother's home, came upon the location where the men held Emmett captive. Curious, he investigated and witnessed the savage beating and pistol-whipping. Till had also been flogged. One of the men, the witness reported, then shot Emmitt Till in the head. The two men then stripped Till of his clothing, fastened a 70-pound gin fin to his neck with barbed wire and dumped his body in the Tallahatchie River. Three days later, the mutilated body surfaced, snagged by a tree stump jutting out of the murky waters. Grotesque and disfigured, his formerly jubilant face was now unrecognizable. Wright was only able to identify the body because of a signet right worn by the youth that remained on one finger, and the ring bore the initial L.T. and had belonged to the teen's father, who had passed away ten years before."[64]

This Church of God in Christ youth stands as a martyr in the struggle for Civil Rights in America. The incident pricked the social and humanitarian consciences of many Americans, whites, as well as blacks: for this hideousness exemplified the magnitude of racial prejudice in our country in 1955. Emmett's funeral was held at Roberts Temple Church of God in Christ in Chicago, Illinois, (the mother church of the Church of God in Christ in the state of Illinois.) The newspaper recorded that there were more than 10,000 people standing around the building while Bishop Louis Henry Ford preached his eulogy. Bishop Ford would forty years later become the third in session as a national leader to

The Triumph of the Black Church

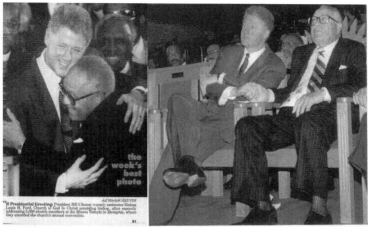

1994, Ebony Magazine President Bill Clinton & Presiding Bishop L.H. Ford

1993, White House Ford, President, Hillary Clinton, Bishop Ford was good personal friends with President Bill Clinton he was only preacher in America at that time who stayed at the White House for more one day visits. Second picture L-R, 1990, Bishop Sanders, Presiding Bishop L.H. Ford, Elder Elijah Hill, and Bishop Ford invited Hill to speak before his College graduates. Bishop Ford was a great lover of COGIC history he encouraged Hill to study

In 1995, Bishop Ford brings the President of the United States he is the first African American national leader to have a sitting President to visit their national meeting.

Bishop Charles Harrison Mason.[65] African Americans and whites heard the moving eulogy rendered by Bishop Louis Henry Ford who was also Bishop Mason's national public relations director at Memphis, Tennessee. People were outraged and shocked over this atrocity. Many people throughout the United States felt that this event was appalling. This travesty was a great injustice and purposed in their hearts that this young man's death by them becoming more motivated to participate in the advancement of the civil rights of African Americans in America.

On February 21, 1965, the assassination of Malcolm X took place. Many of the churches and religious leaders in New York were afraid of the repercussions from the Nation of Islam. It was very difficult to get a church to host Malcolm's funeral service. The Church of God in Christ one of their churches stepped forward threats to hosts his funeral it was the Faith Temple Church of God in Christ, in Brooklyn, New York (now known as Childs Memorial). Malcolm's funeral services was held there, despite the apprehensions of most African American religious leaders at that time.[66]

Another monumental event that took place at Mason Temple in Memphis, Tennessee, was the visit from Dr. Martin Luther King to rally for the sanitation workers. While Dr. King was staying at the Lorraine Hotel, he held his rally at the famous Mason Temple Headquarters of the Church of God in Christ. And his message that night would be, "I've Been to the Mountain Top." It was would be his last speech to the world, it was as if he was prophesying his death; for he proclaimed, "I may not get there with you, but we as a people will get to the promise land." The next day an assassin's bullet killed Dr. Marin Luther King on the balcony of the Lorraine Hotel only a half a mile from the Church of God in Christ World Headquarters where he gave his last speech the night before. Many people were looking forward to Dr. Martin Luther King's sanitation workers march, but this unimaginable crime occurred shaking both white and black America to the core.[67]

The Triumph of the Black Church

1962, Dr. King & Malcolm X Malcolm X COGIC hosted funeral at Childs NY

Present Mason Temple 2012   Prayer Hall to Bishop Mason's Tomb

Bishop Mason 1951   Bishop Mason's body Entombed at Temple

In 1934, the first National Temple built called The Old Tabernacle

The historical Mason Temple was one of the largest facilities owned by African Americans. Bishop C.H. Mason is entombed at this very cite. He was the symbol of the pre-Civil Rights movement in America, forty years before Dr. Martin Luther King, Jr. In 1994, while Bishop Louis Henry Ford of Chicago, Illinois, was Presiding Bishop Worldwide of the Church of God in Christ. Ford invited President Bill Clinton was to Mason Temple to see the location where Dr. Martin Luther King, Jr., gave his last speech to the world. The federal government as part of the occasion was acknowledging the Historic Mason Temple as a national landmark.[68] The President was overwhelmed to learn that it was at the Church of God in Christ Headquarters that Dr. King spoke his famous last speech to America. He as President of the United States sat in the church where Dr. Martin Luther King Jr., sat in the night before his assassination in Memphis, Tennessee.

Bishop Charles Harrison Mason, who was one of America's premier civil liberties activists and founder of COGIC, died in November 17, 1961, at the age of ninety-five years old in Harper's Hospital, Detroit, Michigan. His legacy will endure until the return of our Lord Jesus Christ. Our lives are far better because of men like him who were giants in the Gospel of Jesus Christ.

Bishop Charles Harrison Mason born September 8, 1966 to November 17, 1961 this book is dedicated to his Pre-Civil Rights history in America exposing his lost history and historical contribution to Civil liberties, Civil Rights and Social and Political Justice for all Americans.

END NOTES

Chapter 6: Struggles and Accomplishments During World War I and World War II

1. Vincent Phillip Munoz. (2008). *The Original Meaning of the Free Exercise Claus: The Evidence From The First Congress*. Harvard Journal of Law & Public Policy, 31(3), 1083-1120.
2. Stephen Holmes, (2005)."Dismal Precedents". *New Republic, 232*(7), 31-37.
3. Ibid. Page 31.
4. Donald A. Giannella. (1967). "Religious Liberty, Nonestablishment, and Doctrinal Development". *Harvard Law Review, 80*(7), 1381.
5. Rudra Tamm. (1999). "Religion Sans Ultimate: A Re-Examination of Church-State Law". *Journal Of Church & State, 41*(2), 253-284.
6. Theron F. Schlabach & Richard T. Hughes. (1987). *Proclaim Peace: Christian Pacifism from Unexpected Quarters.* Illinois: University of Illinois Press. Page 60.
7. U.S. War Department & Federal Bureau of Investigation Files, Charles H. Mason Files Investigation Violating the Espionage Act.
8. Charles H. Pleas, "Fifty Years of Achievement: Church of God in Christ", Privately Published: Kansas City, KS, 1955. Page 17.
9. *Word and Witness* 8;10 (Dec 20, 1912):1.
10. Clemmons, I. C. (1996). *Bishop C.H. Mason and the Roots of the Church of God in Christ.* California: Pneuma Life Publishing. Page 127.
11. Holmes, S. (2005). "Dismal Precedents". *New Republic, 232*(7), 31-37.
12. U.S. War Department & Federal Bureau of Investigation Files, Charles H. Mason Files Investigation Violating the Espionage Act.
13. William B. Holt 1917. *A Brief Historical and Doctrinal Statement & Rules for Government of the Church of God in Christ*. Memphis, TN. Page 10.
14. U.S. War Department & Federal Bureau of Investigation Files, Charles H. Mason Files Investigation Violating the Espionage Act. Agent Claude McCaleb report to Bureau, July 15, 1918; OG245662, RG65, BI, NA.
15. James Courts, *The History and Life Work of Bishop C.H. Mason*, Privately Published: Memphis, TN, 1919. Page 36.
16. Ibid. Page 36.
17. Ibid. Page 37.
18. Ibid. Page 38.
19. Ibid. Page 38.
20. Theron F. Schlabach & Richard T. Hughes. (1987). *Proclaim Peace: Christian Pacifism from Unexpected Quarters.* Illinois: University of Illinois Press. Page 65.
21. U.S. War Department & Federal Bureau of Investigation Files, Charles H.

Mason Files Investigation Violating the Espionage Act.

22. Holmes, S. (2005). "Dismal Precedents". *New Republic, 232*(7), 31-37.

23. Ibid. Page 33.

24. U.S. War Department & Federal Bureau of Investigation Files, Charles H. Mason Files Investigation Violating the Espionage Act. Agent Claude McCaleb report to Bureau, July 15, 1918; OG245662, RG65, BI, NA.

25. James Courts, *The History and Life Work of Bishop C.H. Mason*, Privately Published: Memphis, TN, 1919. Page 37.

26. Ibid. Page 37.

27. Ibid. Page 40.

28. Ibid. Page 38.

29. U.S. War Department & Federal Bureau of Investigation Files, Charles H. Mason Files Investigation Violating the Espionage Act. Agent Claude McCaleb report to Bureau, July 15, 1918; OG245662, RG65, BI, NA.

30. U.S. War Department & Federal Bureau of Investigation Files, Charles H. Mason Files Investigation Violating the Espionage Act.

31. Elijah L. Hill. (Copyright year) 2012. Title DVD Recording Follow Peace With All Men. Reproduction of Audio on DVD, Arlington, Texas. Original date of this audio recording was 1950 Bishop Charles Harrison Mason's personal sermon. Memphis, TN.

32. Elijah L. Hill. (Copyright year) 2012. *Title DVD Recording Follow Peace With All Men.* Reproduction of Audio on DVD, Arlington, Texas. Original date of this audio recording was 1950 Bishop Charles Harrison Mason's personal sermon. Memphis, TN.

33. Elijah Hill, *The Azusa Revival, Wrapped in Swaddling Clothes, Lying in a Manger Centennial Edition*" 2006 Independently Published, Page 105.

34. Bishop Ithiel C. Clemmons, *Bishop C.H. Mason and the Roots of the Church of God in Christ,* Publisher: Pneuma Life Publishing, Bakersfield, California, Page 24.

35. James Delk, *He Made Millions Happy* (Hopkinsville, KY: Privately Published, 1950), Page 28.

36. James Courts, *The History and Life Work of Bishop C.H. Mason*, Privately Published: Memphis, TN, 1919. Page 51.

37. *Word and Witness* 8; 10 (Dec 20, 1912):1.

38. U.S. War Department & Federal Bureau of Investigation Files, Charles H. Mason Files Investigation Violating the Espionage Act. Agent Claude McCaleb report to Bureau, July 15, 1918; OG245662, RG65, BI, NA.

39. James Courts, *The History and Life Work of Bishop C.H. Mason,* Privately Published: Memphis, TN, 1919. Page 39.

40. U.S. War Department & Federal Bureau of Investigation Files, Charles H. Mason Files Investigation Violating the Espionage Act. Agent Claude McCaleb report to Bureau, July 15, 1918; OG245662, RG65, BI, NA.

41. James Courts, *The History and Life Work of Bishop C.H. Mason*, Privately

Published: Memphis, TN, 1919. Page 32.

42. Ibid. Page 32.

43. Elijah Hill, *The Azusa Revival, Wrapped in Swaddling Clothes, Lying in a Manger Centennial Edition.* 2006 IPage 105.

44. Minutes of the 12th Annual Holy Convocation, Church of God in Christ, Memphis, TN (November 1919), p. 13-14. "Files of Geraldine Wright", Southfield, Michigan.

45. Theron F. Schlabach & Richard T. Hughes. (1987). *Proclaim Peace: Christian Pacifism from Unexpected Quarters.* Illinois: University of Illinois Press. Page 65.

46. Charles H. Pleas, *Fifty Years of Achievement: Church of God in Christ,* Privately Published: Kansas City, KS, 1955. Page 17.

47. Minutes of the 12th Annual Holy Convocation, Church of God in Christ, Memphis, TN (November 1919), p. 13-14. "Files of Geraldine Wright", Southfield, Michigan.

48. Department of Public Relations Church of God in Christ, comp. *Church of God in Christ Hour Glass Report: Reflections of the Past and Present.* Memphis, TN, n.d., Page 17.

49. *Yes Lord, The Building of Mason Temple, God's Generals: Bishop Riley Williams and Bishop U.E. Miller.* Published Memphis, Tennessee. Page 28.

50. Ibid. Page 28.

51. Ibid. Page 28.

52. Charles H. Pleas, *Fifty Years of Achievement: Church of God in Christ,* Privately Published: Kansas City, KS, 1955. Page 19.

53. Ibid. Page 19.

54. *Yes Lord, The Building of Mason Temple, God's Generals : Bishop Riley Williams and Bishop U.E. Miller.* Published Memphis, Tennessee. Page 24.

55. Charles H. Pleas, *Fifty Years of Achievement: Church of God in Christ,* Privately Published: Kansas City, KS, 1955. Page 20.

56. Department of Public Relations Church of God in Christ, comp. *Church of God in Christ Hour Glass Report: Reflections of the Past and Present.* Memphis, TN, n.d., Page 7.

57. Ibid. Page 8.

58. Ibid. Page 17.

59. James Delk, *He Made Millions Happy* (Hopkinsville, KY: Privately Published, 1950), Page 22.

60. Ibid. Page 22.

61. James L. Delk, *Philosophy and Democracy*, Hopkinsville, KY: Privately Published, 1945. Page 23.

62. Department of Public Relations Church of God in Christ, comp. *Church of God in Christ Hour Glass Report: Reflections of the Past and Present.* Memphis, TN, n.d. Page 12.

63. Minutes of the 12th Annual Holy Convocation, Church of God in Christ,

Memphis, TN (November 1919), p. 13-14. "Files of Geraldine Wright",
Southfield, Michigan.
64. *The Whole Truth. COGIC Youth Emmett Till: The Eternal Symbol of Civil Injustice.* Vol. 1 No. 1. Page 19.
65. Ibid. Page 19.
66. *The Whole Truth. Heritage Edition. COGIC in African American History.* Vol. XXXIII, No. II. Page 3.
67. Ibid. Page 3.
68. Bishop Ithiel C. Clemmons, *Bishop C.H. Mason and the Roots of the Church of God in Christ*, Publisher: Pneuma Life Publishing, Bakersfield, California, Page 133.

Epilogue

This is the autobiography of Prophet Elijah L. Hill the writing of this book for me was to obey God's heavenly vision. When I was on a three day fast in 1989 in Omaha, Nebraska and I saw Bishop Charles Harrison Mason in the vision, and he told me to research and preserve the history of the Church of God in Christ. Going back into my past where it starts with is with my mother and father. My father's name was Ernest Eugene Hill, born in 1937 in Batesville, Arkansas, to Hershel Hill. My father really, did not know his dad he lived in Little Rock, Arkansas, and my father's mother who was my grandmother was Clementine Magnus. My mother's name was Mary Magdalene Murphy/ Hill, and Murphy was her maiden name she was born in December 12, 1938 in Kenansville, North Carolina.

On my father's side of his family they moved from Arkansas to Omaha, Nebraska when he was a couple of years old, and on my mother's side moved from Kenansville, North Carolina to Omaha, Nebraska later when she was a six years old. My mother's mom was Alberta Lee White-Murphy who married John Lee White from Omaha, Nebraska who was stationed in the military in North Carolina who met my grandmother Alberta Lee White, and they were married and moved to Omaha, Nebraska. My grandmother had mother by James R. Bryant when she was only sixteen the same scenario as Clementine who had my father at the early age of sixteen, and both my mother and father moved away from their fathers geographically.

My spiritual journey and experience as a child started with my parents who first came to the Lord Ernest and Mary. When I was born they were already saved and filled with the Holy Spirit. In 1959, directly after they gotten married after High School in Omaha, Nebraska in 1955 my father went into the Korean War.

My Father Ernest Hill 18yrs   Mom Mary Magdalene Hill   Elijah L. Hill

1964, Omaha, Nebraska L-/R, Anita, Trina, Ernest, Elijah, Denise, Renee, Mom

It was a situation for about three years that they really spent a lot of time fasting and praying. I remember those days after this three-year period that my mother and father got divorced when I was three years old.

Therefore, my mother raised the rest of her six children Anita Gail Hill, Trinia Hill, Ernest Hill, Elijah L. Hill, Denise Hill, and Renee Hill. My mom as a single parent raised us all. My mother continued in her fasting and prayer life that she and my father started out with, she ended up spending a lot of time staying up late nights praying, and seeking God many times, I would hear her as a child up late night crying and whaling before the Lord.

This had a lot to do with my spiritual influence and sense of fasting and prayer because my mother spent a lot of time in fasting and prayer, and so this strongly affected my life. My mother came to prominence as a social advocate and humanitarian within the Omaha community as a missionary to the local African American community. She was a great humanitarian in the city of Omaha in the late 1960's during the era of the race riots from 1964-1968.

She had a mission within the African American community in the city of Omaha, Nebraska called Moses and the Ten Commandments Fellowship Mission that she had started around 1964. One of the things that she provided for the community was she acquired food to feed the hungry and she developed a relationship with the Jewish community who gave her many cloths to give away to those in our community that needed it. My mother had a great relationship with Mrs. Blufkins who was a multimillionaire that founded the national furniture chain the Nebraska Furniture Mart in the late 1960s and throughout the early 1980s. Mrs. B, the Omaha community called her admired my mother's vision to help others when she had her six small children to raise as a single parent. She helped to connect my mother with other prominent individuals within the Omaha Jewish community to help my mother to access many properties along 24th and Lake Streets to house three different storehouses of food and cloths.

Mom ended up after Dr. Martin Luther King's assassination in 1968-she felt that God wanted her to go up to Atlanta to be an encouragement to Coretta Scott King. Her heart when out to her having become single parent with her small children she could relate to her plight. At the leading of the Lord my mother took all six of her children she sold all her properties, and we moved up to Atlanta, Georgia she felt she was on a mission to be an encouragement to Coretta Scott King during this difficult time in her life.

She really did not know how she was going to meet Coretta she just trusted God and believed that God was sending her there for this purpose. She ended up getting things establish through a friend of hers she know lived there, and she finally no more than a few weeks met with Coretta Scott King. She shared with her the reason she had come to Atlanta.

Coretta Scott King was touched by my mother's courage to go by the leading of God with all of her small six children as a single parent. I remember going to Ebenezer Baptist Church where Dr. Marin Luther Kings' father was the pastor, Coretta assisted my mother in us getting a place to stay, and she provided groceries for us for several months. The Ebenezer Baptist Church Coretta had her church family to adopt our family for the Christmas in 1968, and I remember all the toys they brought over to our new apartment in Atlanta, Georgia.

I remembered the reviewing of the body of Dr. Martin Luther King as a boy at eight years old they had his body in a white coffin outside of Ebenezer Baptist Church, and I remember the lines of thousands of people lining up just to pass by his coffin to pay their respects to him. My mother met Coretta on several occasions one time I remember Coretta and my mother standing and talking together at Ebenezer Baptist Church in the Basement when my mother was picking up a box of food. My mother had many prophecies about me her son being a proper child all throughout my childhood, and she shared this with Coretta that day at the church. She asked her while we stood there, "Coretta my son has always received these prophecies about him being a proper child and a prophet do you see that, and Coretta told her yes I can see it on him that he is one of our chosen ones."

This was common within the African American community within our religious tradition that people would almost look for those younger than they were that seemed to have God is calling, destiny, and purpose on their lives. They would many times say they were born with a veil over their face or they were a proper child or a prophet even when they were very young. It seemed, because of the plight of African American people the older generation was looking and praying for someone that God would rise up as a Moses to be a deliverer because of the oppression of our people.

I remember growing up attending different church services with my mom between the age of five and twelve years old, that individuals would come up to me and tell my mother your son is a proper child, he has the anointing over his eyes, or he is going to be a prophet. Many times I myself personally as a child I didn't understand what they were talking about I was too young, but when I see the journey God has brought me through after fifty-two years of my life and thirty-five years doing Gospel ministry I can say that I understand.

During that year and a half that we lived there in Atlanta, Georgia was when my mother wrote her first booklet called, "Sell what you have and give to the Poor." I remember when my mother got the pages and all of her kids was lined up in her apartment we helped put the pages together after she got the copies from a printer. My mother told me later that she had shared her book project with Coretta, and she had Dr. Martin Luther Kings' secretary who at that time was a white individual to help type up some of the pages to this booklet. The other half of the book Coretta's secretary finished it for her before she took it to the printer in Atlanta. This was the first time I had seen an African American write and produce their own publication, and this is what encouraged and inspired me to write at such an early age having written four books at the age of seventeen years old while I was still in High School. By the age of eighteen graduating from Bryant Senior High in South Omaha, I had composed a book on Eschatology on biblical prophecy by the time of my High School graduation. I started preaching around the city of Omaha as a well-known boy evangelist preacher from seventeen years old. When I first started writing on subjects of the Bible, I set an appointment with a professor of English at seventeen years old with one of the Seminaries in Omaha to review my manuscripts of my first three books. It was an older white person who had a Ph.D. in English, and he look at me across that desk and stated, "I have a Ph.D. in English and I have not written any books what makes you think that you can."

When I left that office, I was so discouraged and felt that if he has a Ph.D. in English he knows better than me, so thought to give up on the writing that God showed me that I would do in prayer. I left there with tears in my eyes on my way home so discouraged and I felt totally, as if I had embarrassed myself before this man. I had not even finished High School and had not yet gone to College. I did not even have a car at the time I had rode three buses over to Belleview, Nebraska to go to Grace College of the Bible to attend this meeting.

I got home and fell down on my knees in prayer repenting to God that maybe it was my own pride to believe that he had revealed this to me in prayer. The Holy Spirit spoke so strong in my spirit and said, "If I told you that you will write many books you will it does not matter what a man says you do what I told you to do." From that day forward when it came to writing books or whatever God gave to write, I would never again listen to people rather than listen to what God had commissioned me to do.

In High School, I had a high G.P.A average within the whole school, and I was the only African American that took College Pre-Calculus out of six selected students out of five hundred kids. My math teacher I began to witness to him about Christ he said he was an atheist, but I show him one of my books that I had written and he could not believe it based upon my age. He asked me about how can I be a preacher at such a young age I told him well this coming Monday I am holding a revival in North Omaha. He was shocked I asked him to come, and he did it was a blessing to have one of my High School teachers to attend one of my services at seventeen years old.

During my teenage years at the age of sixteen I began to serve the Lord with all my heart and gave my life to Christ, I was staying with one of my relatives who were not living for Christ. After a year, they were upset at me praying and fasting all the time and reading God's word, they put me out of their home. I became homeless at the age of sixteen because I wanted to serve God, but leaving in tears I knew I had not done anything wrong. I had begun to witness to all my siblings after I came to Christ and one of my sister and her husband came to Christ while I was witnessing to them, and they took me in and I stayed with them for two years while finishing High School.

They put me out I did not have a car or a job to take care of myself, so one day I left North High School and took the bus by faith at sixteen, and I only had enough bus fair to get to downtown Omaha to look for a job. I prayed to God to lead me to find a job after being thrown out of the house for the Gospel sake. I felt lead to get off the bus and I stopped at the corner and saw a restaurant called Bishop's Cafeteria, and I went in to fill out my first application. I filled out the application and had an interview with the Manger of Bishop's Cafeteria in 1976 at sixteen years old.

He was a white man he told me that he did not have any positions open, and I knew I was desperate because of having been made homeless recently. It came to me to tell him, "Sir I know you may not have any positions available right now, but if you do have any open please call me because I am a Christian and I will be faithful to your company more than other young people would not having a commitment to Christ." I left there that day knowing I did not have even bus far to get home to my sisters apartment 10 miles away, but I walked there with my heart heavy praying to God to help me in my situation.

That Manger called me back within two days and he offered me a position with my first job at the age of sixteen, and this is how I paid for my cloths, books, and writing material for High School through ninth to eleventh grades. I was determined that two things I would not allow to happen to me no matter what I outcome is that I would not leave my commitment to Christ and I would be the first of my six siblings to graduate from High School.

We moved back to Omaha, Nebraska after my grandmother that lived in Omaha, Nebraska Alberta Lee White kept pleading with my mother to return to Omaha, because she had never been separated from her daughter and her grandchild. We attended Holy Ghost Temple Church of God in Christ the Pastor was Pastor Mack Reed, and my grandparents attended an independent Pentecostal church called Holy Ghost Revival Fellowship Church the Pastor then was Pastor John T. Smith. Sometimes my mother attended church with my grandmother we would attend there as well as Holy Ghost Temple Church of God in Christ in Omaha, Nebraska.

When we came back to Omaha, Nebraska this is when some tragic things occurred in my mother's life that changed our future for the rest of our lives. The state of Nebraska attempted to take us from our mother, and there was a lot of conspiracy involved in the outcome of the case, but even before this case when she came back from Atlanta, there was a contract put out on her life. This person came into my mother's life as someone to help her when she got back in town, put they ended up instead of killing my mother pursuing a relationship with her.

He would break into our house and beat up my mother one time with a blackjack where I was standing there and blood was all over the house. I was sick from the trauma in the hospital for a week at ten years old because of this experience. While in the hospital I could not eat and every time I saw blood, I would go into a coma state. From the age of ten years old to eighteen years old if I saw the sight of blood this would happen to me, and I joined the Marines Corps Reserves to pay for my College education after High School because I had no family support after the courts took all six of us from our mother.

I went to boot camp and one of the medics was taking my blood, and the needle went through my vein, and my blood shoot all over the room like that experience with my mother at ten. I blackout while fainting I prayed to God, and said "Lord please don't let this condition from my childhood last cause them to discharge me from the military and I won't have the money to complete my education." It was my desire so bad to get my College education since I had come through High School without any parental support for three years, and just by the strength of my own volition without parental oversight. That day God answered my prayers when the medics took me back to another room, and I came out of that blackout state, and never experienced this reliving of that moment like that again.

I really believe because of the state of our nation at the time with the Hoover's administration that they were watching my mother and her closeness to Coretta Scott King. Within my mother's pamphlet book called, "Sale what you have and give to the Poor," she had mentioned two pages dealing with the president and America being a nation deceived. I know during that era things said about the President were suspicious by the Hoover administration as communistic if you said anything or spoke your mind publicly.

My mother was in hiding for several years and this individual was terrorizing her, and the community knew this person was very violent and the people loved my mother, so they had this other man to live with her for her protection. He ended up killing that person by cutting his throat. This man broke into our home with a sawed off shoot gun broke down the door, and came in threatening my mother with the gun.

This individual pursued my mother to have a relationship with her telling her to go with him, and he would not fulfill the contract that was placed upon her life. He forced himself in our house and kept my mother under threats with his guns and knives constantly mentioning he would kill her if she went to the police. There are several times she went to the police about this person, but for some reason he would be bonded out and he would continue his threats. My mother had never experienced anything like this, and I was standing right next to her when he pointed the gun at her to shoot her. My mother picked me up and placed me in front of the sawed off shoot gun she was so frightened it was a quick moments reaction.

After my mother was being terrorized for three years then the courts tried to take us from her and they did, and made us wards of the state of Nebraska stating that my mother never could have her children back again. My mother had a nervous breakdown from all the pressure the one thing that hurt her most was her six children being taken away from her. This reminded me of a repeat of history in Omaha, Nebraska with Malcolm X who was born and raised in Omaha, Nebraska thirty years before myself and how because his father taught by Marcus Garvey the Ku Klux Klan came and killed him. Then they blotted to use the welfare system to investigate his mother to prove she was unfit, to take, away her children. After the death of her husband who was Malcolm father, and all the pressure from her not understanding how the system could be justified in taking her children she had a nervous breakdown.

I met an attorney in Omaha, Nebraska when I was around twenty-two years old at a Bible bookstore. She told me your name is Elijah Hill I said yes. She said, "I remember your mother was her name Mary Hill, and I said yes that is my mother. I asked her how she met my mother she told well it was not under good circumstances, and I asked her to share it with me.

She told me it was a long time ago about fifteen years ago when she just got out of law school, and she was assigned to represent my mother in the court case of you all being taken from her. I told her I always wanted to go back to find out what had happened, and she told me Rev. Hill it was so much conspiracy surrounding that case and the accusation. I was new as an attorney straight-out of College I saw the authorities influencing the way that court case would end up. Actually Rev. Hill there was nothing your mother could have been able to do to keep her children they had it all planned for her to lost that battle.

It was in 1990 that the Lord began to deal with me surrounding the pioneers of the 20th Century Pentecostal Movement. Bishop McDaniel had just passed, and the national Church of God in Christ was deciding on who would be selected as the next Bishop of the Church of God in Christ in Nebraska. Several pastors were in the running for the position, so Presiding Bishop L.H. Ford appointed Bishop P.A. Brooks of Michigan to be interim Bishop until the decision was finalized. Bishop Vernon Richardson, the pastor of Faith Temple C.OG.I.C. He was the eldest candidate and had served as a pastor the longest in Nebraska.

I pastored my own church at the time. I had been praying about the next leadership for the jurisdiction, when God showed me that pastor Richardson would be the next Bishop of Nebraska. Many of the younger men did not want Pastor Richardson to be Bishop; they wanted a younger man to take the position. I went over to pastor Richardson's house that weekend, and I told him that God showed me that the national church would select him as the next bishop of Nebraska. He stated to me, "Are you sure son." I told him, standing in his living room I knew that for a surety it would happen just as God had shown me.

It was six months later that the international presiding Bishop L.H. Ford returned back to Nebraska to select from a pool of eight people a bishop for Nebraska. In September of 1991, pastor Vernon Richardson was selected as the next Bishop of Nebraska. Bishop Richardson asked me what I wanted to do in the jurisdiction, and I asked him to allow me to be the historian for the state of Nebraska. He gave me the appointment three months later after his first jurisdictional organizational meeting. I was humbled that the Lord allowed me to tell Bishop Richardson what God had in store for his future.

Following that incident, I entered into several days of fasting, I had a vision that the Late Bishop C.H. Mason and Mother Lizzie Robinson were telling me to research their history and make sure that the younger generations knew about the foundation they laid in the church. It surprised me when I awoke from the vision; I thought, "How could I have had this conversation with these two pioneers who had passed away forty to fifty years ago?" Nevertheless, I knew God had allowed me to see what I saw. I was instructed to research the contributions of the woman that worked alongside the founder, Bishop C.H. Mason. As I began my research, I discovered she lived in Omaha, Nebraska for most of her tenure as the first international supervisor of women for the Church of God in Christ.

Pastor Mack Reed   Press Confer. Presiding Bishop Ford & Mayor Omaha

1994, L-R, Elijah Hill Pastor Mack Reed 1994, L-R, My mom Mary Hill, Bishop Richardson

1999, L-R, Elijah Hill, Wife Cathy Hill,   1993, Omaha, Nebraska L-R, Elijah Hill, wife Cathy
Presiding Bishop C.D.Owens   Mother Louis Secret, Bishop Vernon Richardson

1990, L-R, Bishop Sanders, Presiding Bishop Ford, second photo gave Presiding Bishop
Ford award shaped in the State of Nebraska, and third photo, 1993, Omaha, Nebraska
L-R, Presiding Bishop Ford, Elder Elijah Hill, Bishop Vernon Richardson, Pastor Ford

At a press conference at the Red Lion Inn, the Rev. Louis H. Ford of Chicago said Omaha is a key player in the effort. "Omaha can do more to bring us back to where we want to go than any other city in America," Ford said. "That's because the (church's) roots are so deeply planted and woven together here." Omaha was home to Lizzie Robinson, who Ford said was one of the church's "pioneering ladies."

In 1906, Mrs. Robinson helped the denomination's founder, Bishop Charles H. Mason, organize and structure the church. She was the first supervisor of women's auxiliaries. From modest beginnings in Lexington, MS, the Church of God in Christ has grown to 3.7 million members in 52 countries. But it has forgotten its traditional constituency, the disenfranchised, Ford said. "What did our church specialize in back then? He asked. "Grass-roots people." The church preaches a mix of Pentecostalism and entrepreneurship, training its converts in the ways of business as well as in the ways of God.

"The Church of God in Christ has always been a church that believed in economic development," Ford said. "The church works from the top down (God) and from the bottom up (business). During the Great Depression, for example, the church taught people to farm, to sew, to run businesses. In Memphis, a black-owned bank financed farmers and other entrepreneurs when times got tough.

Today, Ford said the church needs "to be the example for returning back to the roots of the real black church of America that lives for the people, by the people." We're going to stop turning our heads on the dope addicts, the prostitutes, "he said. With a "little bit more love, a little bit more care." Ninety percent can be brought to Christ, he said.

Church of God in Christ, Inc.
World Headquarters
Memphis, Tennessee USA

Office of the Presiding Bishop

Proclamation

WHEREAS: Our Late Founder, Bishop Charles Harrison Mason, envisioned the magnitude of including the women of THE CHURCH OF GOD IN CHRIST, INC., that they were in need of organization and direction while the National Church was in its stage of infancy, and;

WHEREAS: Our Late Mother Lizzie Robinson was appointed as the First General Supervisor of Women of THE CHURCH OF GOD IN CHRIST by our Founder, Bishop Charles Harrison Mason, in and around 1906, and;

WHEREAS: Due to the rapid growth of the Church and Mother Robinson's God-given skills in organizing, she gave great direction and support to the National Women's Work, by creating auxiliaries such as the Bible Band, Sewing Circle, Home and Foreign Mission, Sunshine Band, Purity Class, State Mothers Unit and Secretaries Unit. Also, she prayerfully selected and appointed a host of choice women, many of whom were sent to different States in the United States to be helpers to the Overseers (Bishops) that were appointed by our Founding Father, and;

WHEREAS: Mother Robinson hailed from the great City of Omaha, Nebraska, and she resided there until the date she was promoted to glory in the month of December 1945 while attending the National Convocation in Memphis, Tennessee, and;

BE IT THEREFORE RESOLVED:

Bishop Vernon Richardson has appointed a State Historian in the State of Nebraska in order to research and verify that which will enhance the history of the CHURCH OF GOD IN CHRIST in the State of Nebraska under the auspices of Elder Elijah Hill and by will of the CHURCH OF GOD IN CHRIST there in Omaha, Nebraska;

BE IT FINALLY RESOLVED:

That the eight day of July in this year of our Lord, one thousand nine hundred and ninety-two be a DAY OF MEMORIAL to honor the life and work of Mother Lizzie Robinson, the First National Supervisor who has fallen asleep in Jesus.

Given under my hand and the Seal of the Presiding Bishop at World Headquarters in the City of Memphis, Tennessee, this 27th day of March in the year of our Lord one thousand nine hundred and ninety-two.

1992, Omaha, Nebraska Presiding Bishop L.H. Ford gave me a Proclamation for recovering the history of Mother Lizzie Robinson, for being the Church of God in Christ historian for the state of Nebraska

The church needs to open child care centers all across America, halfway houses and shelters in every large city, and "get boys and girls to (the farm) to make them see livestock, let them plant fruit trees, teach them to be builders." Let's open some stores, stop marching and put the money to working," he said. "That's what our church is all about.

In the spiritual arena, Ford said, the church also needs to get down to business. It needs to carry Jesus message of salvation out into the streets. "We still believe in all-night prayer, fasting, praying, clapping our hands and stomping our feet and screaming, "He said." We will not run from our responsibilities in the community."

The next event that took place was when we came up before the city board to review whether the mother church of Nebraska was significant of being a historic landmark recognized by the civic authorities. The church that was named after her and her husband was selected to be historical site by the city board because of Mother Robinson's historic and international significance. I submitted the information to

Bishop Richardson then told him that we needed to get the national church involved. I wrote another article to go in the Whole Truth Paper about the civic authorities recognizing Mother Lizzie Robinson's church as a historic landmark. The article was published in the worldwide Whole Truth Newspaper.
The city planning department helped me organize my argument to the Federal Registry of Historic places to request their recognition of Mother Lizzie Robinson as a significant figure in the history of America. It took about six to eight months following our preparation of the nomination application.

After its preparation, I had to first travel to Lincoln, Nebraska to convince the State Historical Society to vote to allow the nomination to proceed to Washington, D.C.

Bishop Urges Church of God in Christ to Return to Roots

By Julia McCord
World-Herald Staff Writer

The presiding bishop of the Church of God in Christ on Friday called on the church to go back to its roots in order to secure the future.

At a press conference at the Red Lion Inn, the Rev. Louis H. Ford of Chicago said Omaha is a key player in the effort.

"Omaha can do more to bring us back to where we want to go than any other city in America," Ford said. "That's because the (church's) roots are so deeply planted and woven together here."

Omaha was home to Lizzie Robinson, who Ford said was one of the church's "pioneering ladies."

In 1906 Mrs. Robinson helped the denomination's founder, Bishop Charles H. Mason, organize and structure the church. She was the first supervisor of women's auxiliaries.

From modest beginnings in Lexington, Miss., the Church of God in Christ has grown to 3.7 million members in 52 countries. But it has forgotten its tradi-

Rudy Smith/World-Herald

Ford ... "The Church of God in Christ has always been a church that believed in economic development."

Bishop Says Omaha Key To His Church

● Continued from Page 65

said. "That's what our church is all about."

In the spiritual arena, Ford said, the church also needs to get down to business. It needs to carry Jesus' message of salvation out into the streets.

"We still believe in all-night prayer, asking, praying, clapping our hands and stomping our hands and screaming," he said, "We will not run from our responsibilities in the community."

66   OMAHA WORLD-HERALD   Saturday, September 21, 1991

tional constituency, the disenfranchised, Ford said.

"What did our church specialize in back then?" he asked. "Grass-roots people."

The church preaches a mix of pentacostalism and entrepreneurship, training its converts in the ways of business as well as in the ways of God.

"The Church of God in Christ has always been a church that believed in economic development," Ford said. "The church works from the top down (God) and from the bottom up (business).

Ford came to Omaha for the 74th Annual Holy Convocation of the Nebraska Jurisdiction, which concludes today.

The northeast and eastern Nebraska jurisdictions recently merged because of the death of one bishop and the illness of another.

Ford said he had come to bring about unity "and begin the real growth with this state."

Bishop P.S. Brooks from Detroit was appointed interim bishop of the newly created jurisdiction in December and will serve until a permanent bishop can be named.

ness).

During the Great Depression, for example, the church taught people to farm, to sew, to run businesses. In Memphis, a black-owned bank financed farmers and other entrepreneurs when times got tough.

Today, Ford said, the church needs "to be the example for returning back to the roots of the real black church of America that lives for the people, by the people."

"We're going to stop turning our heads on the dope addicts, the prosti-

tutes," he said. With a "little bit more love, a little bit more care," 90 percent can be brought to Christ, he said.

The church needs to open child care centers all across America, halfway houses and shelters in every large city, and "get boys and girls to (the farm) to make them see livestock, let them plant fruit trees, teach them to be builders."

"Let's open some stores, stop marching and put the money to working," he said.

Please turn to Page 66, Col. 1

1992, Presiding Bishop L.H. Ford Press Conference Omaha

Rev. Hill Appointed to Landmarks Commission

On November 10, 1992, Mayor P.J. Morgan appointed Rev. Elijah L. Hill to the Landmarks Heritage Preservation Commission for a three-year term. The Mayor officially conducted a swearing-in ceremony for Rev. Hill on July 14, 1993, in the Legislative Chambers of the Omaha/Douglas Civic Center. The Mayor invited Rev. Hill's family to be in attendance.

Rev. Hill had this year been presented with an award from Governor E. Benjamin Nelson for his civic achievement toward the renaissance and preservation of Mother Lizzie Robinson's history. As a result of his local preservation efforts, Erskine Street from 24th to 28th Street was changed to Lizzie Robinson Ave.; two local properties were designated as historic landmarks; and the house associated with Lizzie Robinson was placed on the Federal Registry of Historic Places in April 1993. The National Trust of Historic Preservation, chartered by Congress in 1949 and a non-profit organization with over 250,000 members, has recently selected Rev. Hill to attend the 47th national convention in St. Louis, Mo., September 29-October 3, 1993, with all expenses paid for by the National Trust. The National Trust had been organizing a way to incorporate cultural diversity into their national preservation program. Two years ago they raised funds to bring grassroots minority leaders into a dialogue with hundreds of preservationists from across the U.S. Their objective is to offer those from various cultural backgrounds the opportunity to participate and take back new skills and understanding to community efforts.

Since Rev. Hill has been a commissioner on the Omaha City Commission, he has been made chairman for the subcommittee on cultural diversity, and is presently chairman for the Landmarks Heritage Preservation Commission for the city. Rev. Hill is the pastor of A Way that Of is the center of A Way that Of Way Church of God in Christ.

From (l-r): Mrs. Hill, Rev. Elijah Hill, their two daughters and Mayor P.J. Morgan.

1994, Rev. Elijah L. Hill, appointment by Mayor Omaha His family, Rev. Hill, and Mayor P.J. Morgan

The property that Mother Robinson used to own as her home was currently owned by the city, and they had taken it for taxes not paid after her death. The city told me that the interstate came through that area, her lot was adjacent to the Highway and that the city owned easement rights on the lot.

The only way the property could be taken back was to pay the back taxes, and request that the city planning department release the property for historic reasons. I finally persuaded the city-planning department to release the lot. We did not have any money in the historic committee, since we had just started the jurisdiction.

At this time, the presiding Bishop L.H. Ford was reviving the history of the late founder bishop C.H. Mason. He had, in 1955, gotten a street named after Bishop Mason. He had a national committee formed to research the history of the earlier pioneers of the Church of God in Christ. His focus was on the founder Bishop C.H. Mason, while the Lord told me to work on the history of Mother Robinson. Her history could be easily researched, since she lived in Omaha, Nebraska where I lived at the time. My instructions in prayer were to do everything for Mother Robinson that the national church was doing for the founder, Bishop Mason. Therefore, I came up with a plan to accomplish four things in the area of history for Nebraska:

1. To have a street named after Mother Robinson.

2. To have the first church started by her and her husband protected as a historic landmark.

3. To write a nomination for the last existing home of her daughter placed on the Federal Registry of historical places

4. To purchase the land where Mother Robinson's home used to exist, and build at Museum on it.

THE WHOLE TRUTH

OMAHA REMEMBERS MOTHER ROBINSON

Mayor P.J. Morgan, mayor of Omaha, Nebraska, proclaimed February 27, 1992, "Mother Robinson Day." Elder Elijah Hill served as the driving force to obtain the recognition for one of the true pioneers of the Church Of God In Christ. Along with the day, Elder Hill is attempting to get Mother Robinson's home and former church designated as historic landmarks. In the plan is also a goal to get a portion of Erskine Street renamed Lizzie Robinson Avenue.

Mother Robinson and her husband, Elder Edward Robinson started the first Church Of God In Christ in Nebraska in 1913. Of course, Mother is renown as the first National Supervisor of Women in the Church Of God In Christ. She was appointed by Bishop C.H. Mason and was the lay foundation for one of the strongest entities in the entire Church.

We in the Church know what a great saint and devoted laborer for Christ Mother was, and now the secular world is recognizing her for her many accomplishments. The following is the wording of the official proclamation:

PROCLAMATION

Whereas, Elder Elijah L. Hill state historian and Bishop Vernon Richardson have found through their studies that Mother Lizzie Robinson hailed from the great state of Omaha, Nebraska, until the date she was promoted to glory in December 1945, while attending the National Memphis Convocation; and,

Whereas, the Church Of God In Christ had its beginnings in Nebraska in about 1913, when Mother Robinson and Elder Edward Robinson moved to Omaha and resided at 2864 Corby St., not long after they established the first Gold Cup Award. church in Omaha, located at 2318 N. 26th Street; and,

Whereas, Mother Robinson's God given skills in organizing, gave great direction and support to the National Women's Work organization and she appointed a host of women who were sent through out the United States to help the Bishops that were appointed by their Founding Father.

Now, Therefore, I, P.J. Morgan, Mayor of Omaha, do hereby proclaim July 8, 1992 as

MOTHER ROBINSON MEMORIAL DAY

in Omaha and urge all residents to honor the life and work of Lizzie Robinson.

In Witness Whereof, I have set my hand and caused the Official Seal of the City of Omaha to be affixed this 27th day of February, 1992.

RECORD
REPORTS PAID !!!

The lines were long and the totals for each report seemed to be higher than the amount asked. The bishops and supervisors of the Church Of God In Christ were eager to break the record reports from last year. It became apparent that the record would fall after jurisdiction upon jurisdiction reported. Some jurisdictions were two to three thousand dollars over their quota. One jurisdiction reported 100% over the requested quota; that jurisdiciton was Central Tennessee, Bishop W.L. Porter is prelate.

The initial tally appears to be 3.5 million dollars and possibly going higher. An official accounting will be placed in The Whole Truth's next edition. Hats must be taken off to Bishop L.H. Ford and the General Board of Bishops for such a successful ingathering.

As a special interest story, The Whole Truth will highlight the five highest reports in a coming edition.

UNAC-5 NATIONAL BIBLE COMPETITIC

The United National Auxiliaries' Convention of the Church Of God In Christ announces the National Bible Bowl Competition. This competition is held annually in the UNAC-5 Convention and is designed for the winning team of each Jurisdictional Bible Bowl Competition to compete on a National level for the UNAC-5 Gold Cup Award.

This year the Bible Bowl will cover Church Doctrine (information may be obtained from Understanding Church Doctrine Book and the December 1990-February 1991 YPWW Quarterly), Church History (information obtained from December 1986-February 1987 YPWW Quarterly), and the Entire Book of Psalm. There will also be a Junior Bible Bowl Competition covering the same material and the Book of Psalm, chapters 1-75.

Also, during the UNAC-5 Convention the following ministries will be available: National Spelling Bee Competition, Oratorical Competition, Math/Computer Competition, Drama Workshop, UNAC-5 Young Ladies Workshop, UNAC-5 Gentlemen's Workshop, Miss UNAC Pageant, Youth Talent Hour, and Preacher's Children Workshop.

The topics for the Oratorical Competition are:

fro
hom

3) As v
and
Gos

For
ministry

Bible B
Mrs. He
28812 R
Inkster,
(313) 27

Spelling
Ms. San
14922 S
Harvey,
(708) 33

Drama
Ms. Bre
8501 E.
Kansas
(816) 35

UNAC-
Worksh

In February 27, 1992, the Whole Truth writes up Elder Elijah Hill about obtaining a Proclamation from the City of Omaha, NE, for Mother Lizzie Robinson.

A meeting was arranged at Bishop Richardson's house where the bishop and I talked about my plans for the history of Nebraska. Bishop Richardson was surprised that I had such a great vision when he had just appointed me as the historian. I told Bishop Richardson that God wanted me to accomplish these things during his administration because God wanted him to be recognized by the national church. I told him some of the ministers' thought that if they could sit on him because of his age, they would wear him down, so on day they could take his place.

I told him that God had a plan, at his then age of eight-two, to bless him more in his latter days and to be recognized for the chosen vessel he was. I told Bishop the only thing I asked was that when all this success began to occur that he would back me up with the pastors, because I believed they would try to come between us to stop what God was doing. Bishop Richardson told me he appreciated the plan that God had given me, and that he wanted to pray for me that God would give me the ability to do all that I had in my heart. I wrote a letter to presiding Bishop L.H. Ford; a letter signed by Bishop Richardson, outlining the fact that we wanted to research the historic roots of the Church of God in Christ in Nebraska, and do whatever we could to bring about a renaissance of C.O.G.I.C. history back in our state of Nebraska and me. I told Bishop that it was important that the national church be aware of what our intensions were, so that as things materialized they would give us their support. After I research Mother Robinson's history in detail for six months, I was reading the Whole Truth Newspaper, and I decided to take the history I researched and request a Proclamation from the national church to validate the history.

Bishop gave me the permission to contact the national church. The presiding Bishop's office gladly received the historic information about Mother Lizzie Robinson, and six months later sent us back an official proclamation to Nebraska.

THE WHOLE TRUTH

FIRST AND YOUNGEST BLACK TO CHAIR COMMISSION

Mayor P.J. Morgan, Omaha, NE presents Elder Hill an award with his wife Catherine and daughters, Tiffany and Tamara.

Recently, Elder Elijah L. Hill was made Chair of the Landmarks Heritage Preservation Commission.

The Mayor officially conducted a swearing-in ceremony for Elder Hill on July 14, 1993, in the legislative Chambers of the Omaha/Douglas Civic Center. The Mayor invited Elder Hill's family to be in attendance. Elder Hill has been cited with an award from Governor E. Benjamin Nelson for his civic achievement toward the renaissance and preservation of Mother Lizzie Robinson's history. As a result of his local preservation efforts, Erskine Street from 24th to 28th Street was changed to Lizzie Robinson Ave; two local properties were designated as historic landmarks; and the house associated with Lizzie Robinson was placed on the Federal Registry of Historic Places in April 1993.

The National Trust of Historic Preservation, chartered by Congress in 1949 and a non-profit organization with over 250,000 members, selected Elder Hill to attend their 47th national convention in St. Louis, Mo., September 29 -October 3, 1993, with all expenses paid for by the National Trust.

The National Trust had been organizing a way to incorporate cultural diversity into their national preservation program. Two years ago they raised funds to bring grass-roots minority leaders into a dialogue with hundreds of preservationists

HOMEGOING SERVICES FOR MOTHER CARLEE QUICK

JUNE 25, 1892 - MARCH 23, 1994

"THANK GOD FOR 102 YEARS OF BLESSINGS"

Carlee Quick was born in Bennettsville, South Carolina to Peter and Sylvia Miller Pearson. She grew up with her brothers John Augustus, Daniel and Handy. Her sisters were Sally Ann, Mattie and Laura. Because of her longevity, she has vivid memories of slavery.

She was educated at Laurinburg Institute, among the first students to attend the school. At an early age she accepted Christ as her personal Saviour. Her family church was Smyrna Methodist Church. She married Dwight Quick and moved to his home in Green Pond, North Carolina. She gave birth to ten children: Mozella, Morris and then James preceded her in death.

Mother Quick migrated with her family north to New Jersey. There she worked as a domestic. She also spent several years caring for children in her home. Many children beside her own received the special attention and loving care she was well known for.

Mother Quick was an ardent church worker. At Bethel AME Zion Church in Passaic, New Jersey, she organized an outstanding youth choir. She loved to invite the pastor to join her family at the Sunday afternoon dinner table. She gained quite a reputation as an expert baker. Mother Quick earned thousands of dollars in support of her church and her family by baking cakes and pies. At the age of seventy-six she served as the first cook for the newly organized Grace Temple Day Care Center.

In September 1993, Elder Elijah Hill the Whole Truth writes surrounding Him being appointed by Mayor P.J. Morgan as the first and youngest African American to the Landmarks Heritage Preservation Commission

194

I told Bishop that we had something from my church; in order to make sure no one else purchased it when it came up for sale.

World Headquarters Memphis, Tennessee USA Office of the Presiding Bishop Proclamation:

Whereas: Our Late Founder, Bishop Charles Harrison Mason, envisioned the magnitude of including the women of THE CHURCH OF GOD IN CHRIST, INC., that they were in need of organization and direction while the National Church was in its stage of infancy, and;

Whereas: Our Late Mother Lizzie Robinson was appointed as the First General Supervisor of Women of THE CHURCH OF GOD IN CHRIST by our Founder, Bishop Charles Harrison Mason, in and around 1911, and;

Whereas: Due to the rapid growth of the Church and Mother Robinson's God-given skills in organizing, she gave great direction and support to the National Women's Work, by creating auxiliaries such as the Bible Band, Sewing Circle, Home and Foreign Mission, Sunshine Band, Purity Class, State Mothers Unit, and Secretaries Unit. Also, she prayerfully selected and appointed a hose of choice women, many of whom were sent to different States in the United States to be helpers to the Overseers (Bishops) that were appointed by our Founding Father, and;

Whereas: Mother Robinson hailed from the great City of Omaha, Nebraska, and she resided there until the date she was promoted to glory in the month of December 1945 while attending the National Convocation in Memphis, Tennessee, and;

Be It Therefore Resolved:
Bishop Vernon Richardson has appointed a State Historian in the State of Nebraska in order to research and verify that which will enhance the history of the CHURCH OF GOD IN CHRIST in the State of Nebraska under the auspices of Elder Elijah Hill and by

the will of the CHURCH OF GOD CHRIST there in Omaha, Nebraska;

Be It Finally Resolved:
That the eight day of July in this year of our Lord, one thousand nine hundred and ninety two be a DAY OF MEMORIAL to honor the life and work of Mother Lizzie Robinson, the First National Supervisor who has fallen asleep in Jesus.

Given under my hand and the Seal of the Presiding Bishop at the World Headquarters in the City of Memphis, Tennessee, this 27th day of March in the year of our Lord one thousand nine hundred and ninety two.

L. H. Ford
Presiding Bishop
This proclamation was a way the national church was validating her history, so that when I approached the civic officials, our official document would validate their support. Next, I called the city of Omaha's planning department to find out what the criteria was to change a street name. Then I called the city of Omaha's Historical Landmark Board to find out their qualifications for a property to be placed under their protection as a historic landmark.

I was given the run around many times, but I stayed persistent. If one department held me up with their answer, I would call about my other project. I kept following up with all four projects until progress was made on each one. Once progress was made, I met again with Bishop Richardson, and explained all the details to him to get his input. The national church delayed the proclamation, so I asked Bishop Richardson if he would allow me to speak as his spokesperson to the presiding Bishop about our request, in the capacity as the historian for Bishop's jurisdiction. I called the presiding Bishop's office in Chicago, and I spoke with Presiding Bishop L.H. Ford that next morning.

4

THE WHOLE TRUT

STATE OF NEBRASKA'S GOVERNORS RECOGNITION AWARD

Mother Robinson's actual home was smaller than Ida's home, commonly referred to as the 'big house'. Bishop C.H. Mason would stay at Ida Bakers home and many other of the old pioneers like: Mother Lillian Brooks Coffey.

Bishop Mason preached the funeral of Mother Lizzie Robinson, since she died while at the Memphis Convocation. Mother Dollie M. Matthews, the third state mother of Connecticut

Pictured left to right: Bishop Vernon Richardson, Governor Nelson and Elder Elijah L. Hill.

On February 27, 1993, Bishop Vernon Richardson prelate of Nebraska and Elder Elijah L. Hill received the Governor's Recognition Award, from Governor E. Benjamin Nelson. The award was presented to Bishop Vernon Richardson for his willingness and insight to appoint a historian to establish the rich Nebraskan history of the Church Of God In Christ. Elder Elijah L. Hill, was sighted for his civic achievement towards the renaissance and preservation of Mother Lizzie Robinson's history in the state of Nebraska. The night of the occasion, Governor E. Benjamin had someone to read a personalized letter to Elder Hill, stating that, "This effort speaks well of your dedication to both the State and the Church and you are most deserving of this award". The International Chairman of the General Assembly, Dr. Frank Ellis, was present at the occasion to see the awards presented at the Red Lion Hotel, Ball Room, in Omaha, NE.

Elder Elijah L. Hill has also appeared before the State of Nebraska's Historical Society, on January 8, 1993, in Lincoln, NE., accompanied by Lynn Meyer of the City of Omaha's City planning department. Lynn Meyer is the City of Omaha's Historic Preservation Administrator, who supported Elder Hill's nomination of Ida Baker's former home that is seventy nine years old. Elder Hill made a fifteen minutes slide presentation to the Historical Society's Board, then they voted unani-

presented the last gift from the national women's department. She presented to Mother Robinson a beautiful white satin, princess style dress with pretty pearl buttons down the front. At Mother Robinson's last annual national women's day in Memphis, Tenn., Mother wore her dress. Her daughter, Ida Baker, "big sister" she was called, laid her to rest in it. Mother Lillian Brooks Coffey made sure that everything was in order in finalizing her burial in Omaha, she purchased a beautiful granite head stone that reads "Mother Lizzie Robinson the First General Supervisor of the Women's Department of the Church Of God In Christ", at Mt. Hope Cemetery in Omaha, NE.

"The Lifted Banner", a newsletter established in 1944 by the National Women's Department, was printed and circulated out of Mother Robinson's former home. The newsletter continued for over thirty or more years before it went out of print. We thank Mother Robinson for her untiring love for the growth of the international organization. Before Mother Robinson died, she had the neon sign at International Headquarters nstalled in 1945. Mother Mattie McGlothen had the replica of the Omaha street sign, named after Mother Lizzie Robinson, presented during Women's Day in the 85th Holy Convocation. Mother Mattie McGlothen is one of the last original state mothers who was appointed by the Late First General

In April 1993, Elder Elijah Hill the Whole Truth writes surrounding him and Bishop Vernon Richardson pictured with the Governor of Nebraska giving them the Governor's recognition award.

I explained that we were looking into getting a street named after Mother Robinson to uphold the historic strides he was making with the history of Bishop C.H. Mason. The presiding Bishop assured me that he would have his secretary in Memphis, Tennessee send us the document. He also was having his historical committee make sure that the national church validated all of the information I had submitted. Having these two proclamations in the *Whole Truth Newspaper,* Bishop was pleased with how God was blessing me to prosper in all the things I was putting my hands to do. I knew that the city council would give me problems with the street name change. The city planning director told me, "Rev. Hill, you are setting a precedence; we have never given a street name change to a female, white or black." He assured me that I could attempt it, but that he would not support it when it went to city council. I knew that one angle they would come up with was that the residents that lived along that three-block stretch would not want it changed.

Therefore, I researched all the owners, wrote up a petition and asked them if they would support me by signing the petition when I met with the city council. The Lord blessed me to get all of the owners on both sides of the street to sign the petition, after explaining to them the purpose of the street name was for a historically significant individual to be recognized for their accomplishments. I began to research how we could bring the women's convention to Omaha, Nebraska. The convention and visitors bureau of the city of Omaha did an analysis on the women's convention. They told me that the women convention was 30,000 or more attendees, and that it was too large for the city of Omaha to host. They told me that they did not know of many conventions they had dealt with that was that big.

The analysis from the convention and visitors bureau demonstrated the millions of dollars that would impact the business community if they came here for a week. I asked her to write a letter to the president of the city council, Joe Friend, allowing him to see that the importance of Mother Lizzie Robinson having this type of recognition would be to the city economic advantage. The city council member told me that he had seen the work that I had done for the street name, and that he would make sure at that night of the hearing, we would have the necessary votes to get the street name passed.

Many thought that I would not be able to accomplish the street change. Some of the older people wondered how I could know more about Mother Robinson, when I was not even born before she died. Nevertheless, God had blessed me with the necessary know how to research her information in detail. During research, I traveled to Memphis, TN, and located every document I could that talked about Mother Lizzie Robinson. Some of the documents that I pulled included:

1. Her last will and testament

2. The deed of her home she purchased

3. Her deed of record of the mother church

4. The deed of record of Ida Baker's home

5. I traced her daughter by finding her name in the cross-city directory from 1912 to 1925.

Piece by piece like a puzzle I was able to fit together the pattern of history of this great humanitarian.
Bishop L.H. Ford was about to be up for reelection as presiding bishop. I had submitted a resolution to the National churches General Assembly to approve a one-day holiday for the first general mother to be recognized by the national church. The resolution was not allowed to go to the General Assembly. I got word that it needed to go past the presiding bishop before it went to the General Assembly.

1999, KC, MO, L-R, Jackson, Bishop Newton, Elder Elijah Hill, Presiding Bishop Owens

1997,Barker Temple Hill Family, 2nd pic Mayor Morgan, Hill, Richardson, ect

1994, Chairman of General Assembly Ellis, Hill, wife Cathy, Hill awards

2007, Hill Prophesied Bishop Blake winning election, Bishop P.A. Brooks, Bishop Brooks daughter, Elder Elijah Hill at Bishop Blake election Celebration

Bishop L.H. Ford asked my Bishop, Vernon Richardson, to speak on Saturday at the International Holy Convocation. He told me he had never had this kind of an opportunity in all his sixty years of preaching in the Churches of God in Christ. I told Bishop Richardson this was what God was showing me when I first started two years ago: that he would be blessed beyond his expectation when it came to being recognized by the national church.

I took Bishop Richardson to Lincoln, Nebraska with me to introduce him to Governor Ben Nelson. He told me, "Son you going to take me to meet the governor of Nebraska?" I told him the governor was going to give me an award for bringing about a renaissance of the history of Mother Lizzie Robinson. This would be a good time for him to take a picture with the govern, and we could send to the Churches Whole truth Newspaper. This would show the national church that we were being progressive on getting the secular world to acknowledge the history of the Church of God in Christ.

Elder Robert Alexander, who was the foster son of Ida Baker, Mother Lizzie Robinson's only daughter, gave me a lot of information about Mother Robinson. I interviewed several individuals to match together the consistence of the testimony. Individuals I interviewed for this book over fourteen years of research Included: Bishop B.T. McDaniel, Mother Lillian Chambers, Mother McDaniel's, Bishop Vernon Richardson, Sister Naomi V. Lewis, Mother Franklin, Flenroy Barker, Victor Barker.

The Triumph of the Black Church

CONTACT INFORMATION FOR BOOK ORDERS

Mail Order

Elijah Hill
P.O. Box 180412
Arlington, Texas, 76096
Call 760-278-3157

On-Line Personal Site

www.elijahlhill.com
www.cogicmuseum.org

To order all of Elijah Hill's books

Women Come Alive
(Biography of Mother Lizzie Robinson)

The Azusa Street Revival, Wrapped in
Swaddling Clothes Lying in Manger
(Biography of William J. Seymour)

The Triumph of The Black Church
(Biography of Bishop Charles Harrison Mason)

Other Outlets
Call your local Bible Book Store to Place an Order

Amazon.com

The Triumph of the Black Church